THIS ROCK 'N' ROLL WON'T LAST YOU KNOW!

John Verity

THIS ROCK 'N' ROLL WON'T LAST YOU KNOW!

John Verity

WYMER PUBLISHING
Bedford, England

First published in Great Britain in 2023
by Wymer Publishing
www.wymerpublishing.co.uk
Tel: 01234 326691
Wymer Publishing is a trading name of Wymer (UK) Ltd

Copyright © 2023 John Verity / Wymer Publishing.
This edition 2024.

ISBN: 978-1-915246-61-5
(also available in eBook)

Edited by Jerry Bloom

The Author hereby asserts his rights to be identified
as the author of this work in accordance with sections
77 to 78 of the Copyright, Designs & Patents Act 1988.

All rights reserved. No part of this publication may be
reproduced or transmitted in any form or by any means,
electronic or mechanical, including photocopying, or any
information storage and retrieval system, without written
permission from the publisher.

This publication is sold subject to the condition that it shall not,
by way of trade or otherwise, be lent, re-sold, hired out or
otherwise circulated without the publishers prior consent in any
form of binding or cover other than that in which it is published
and without a similar condition including this condition
being imposed on the subsequent purchaser.

Every effort has been made to trace the copyright holders of the
photographs in this book but some were unreachable. We would
be grateful if the photographers concerned would contact us.

Typeset by Andy Bishop / Tusseheia Creative.
Printed by CMP, Dorset, England.

A catalogue record for this book is available from the British Library.

Cover design: Tusseheia Creative
Front cover image © Lee Scriven

Contents

Forewords		7
	Rod Argent	
	Del Bromham	
	Graham Oliver	
	John Gordon	
	Chris White	
	Bob Henrit	
Preface		11
1	Sellars Fold	13
2	On The Move	19
3	The Plan	23
4	Best Laid Plans…	29
5	Back To Bradford	33
6	New Horizons 1968	39
7	The Colonies	45
8	The New World	53
9	Time To Go Home	61
10	At Last!	69
11	The Reality Check	75
12	New Horizons	83
13	Ch-Ch- Changes	91
14	More Ch-Ch- Changes!	109
15	Friends	127
16	Into The Future…	129
17	The Fire	131
18	Back To Reality	135
19	On The Move Again	141
20	Guilt Is A Heavy Load…	147
21	The Tricky Truck	149
22	Here We Go Again…	159
23	A Fresh Start	171
24	I Get Knocked Down, But…	183
25	All Change	201
26	A Shock On The Horizon	207
27	A Welcome Surprise	215
28	New Horizons	219
29	Not Quite 'The End'	223

For Mum and Dad

Forewords

John became a member of Argent in 1974, for the last year and a half or so of its existence, after Russ amicably split with us to concentrate more on his songwriting and solo work.

Coincidentally, we'd only just finished a tour with John as support, but in fact had known him and been aware of his magnificent voice and soulful guitar playing for years. This made it a quite natural choice to ask whether he might fancy joining us as a bona-fide member of the band. We also knew what a really lovely guy he was, (and believe me, such things are really important when a band is constantly touring!)

To our delight he immediately said yes, and along with another new addition, the talented young jazz-informed guitarist John Grimaldi, we moved forward in a new five-piece formation. John became a real friend and good fun on the road, particularly through the period of arduous touring that we undertook immediately we started with our new lineup, and by the end of 1975 we had also completed two brand new albums, *Circus* and *Counterpoints* — (the latter being produced by Tony Visconti) in our extremely creative final period!

All good things do come to end though, and we all moved on to different things. John has never, though, retreated from being a really fine musician — in the last few years I've had the pleasure of catching him several times in concert and I have to say his voice and powerful guitar playing are undiminished!

Rod Argent, 2023

The life of a musician and the world one inhabits is totally different from any other profession I can think of. Full of highs one day and tumbling down to mind crushing lows the next. Finding oneself in scenarios that many outside the business would not believe!

"Oh he is making it up", they might cry! Despite all that, a true musician carries on, for no-one believes in their art and creativity like a musician does. One such musician is John Verity.

Although I knew of his existence for many years, it is only in the past couple of years that I have really got to know him.

To quote a phrase 'we were like ships in the night', meeting up at various festivals and multi bills around the UK. However, we never got involved in long conversations then, something he and I now find ourselves doing in private, which could gain marathon status.

John has many stories to tell, and I have often suggested he should write a book; to which he would respond that no-one would be interested or moreover no-one would believe the stories. I completely understand that as I went through the same dilemma when I eventually wrote my autobiography.

I don't think John realises how talented he is. He has a great voice and is a pretty fine guitarist. As well as being a fine musician not only as a solo artist but as a session guitarist, recording engineer and record producer working with some very reputable artists. You don't need me to tell you, read on because he can tell you much better than I.

Finally, on a personal level, I often wonder what might have happened had we met many years ago? Although being born in opposite ends of the UK, some of our situations we have found ourselves in and people we have met are pretty much the same.

We are having a lot of fun with our new musical project The Verity Bromham Band (it took ages to think of that name… ha ha!).

However, I'd like to think we have grown quite close as human beings and if our musical bond should end tomorrow, I would like to think our friendship will continue for many years to come.

Del Bromham, Stray, Verity Bromham Band

I first saw John Verity in my local club, it was Sunday, and he was sporting the first *Gibson SG Custom* I had ever seen. I dashed to the pay phone in the club to call Steve Dawson and told him you have to see this band.

It was 1973 and I had little idea John would be a foundation to my career spanning over forty years.

In 1976 the band I was in recorded demos at a studio in London, John was facilitating this endeavour, and I was recently handicapped with a serious injury to my left index finger. John painstakingly allowed me to do a few notes at a time dropping me in for each part and comping it all together, for which I will be eternally grateful.

More than he ever knew, he was giving me hope I could do this. John produced the first Saxon album, and we learnt a lot from this recording at Livingston studio.

John was an integral part in the founding of Saxon and a vital part of the success of Saxon whom without laying those cornerstones at the beginning with his help, history may have been much different.

I have to say thank you John V producer, engineer, and fantastic singer guitarist and songwriter for helping me make music a lifelong career.

Graham Oliver, guitarist and founder member of Saxon

Back when the only way to make your voice sound in tune was to… er… sing in tune, and guitar amplifiers used components Marconi would have recognised, there was John Verity — 'JV' to his many friends and followers.

And he's still there, rocking audiences with that high clear vocal that would shame many, more hyped warblers, and wringing lush tones from a signature guitar — always professional, always with passion.

I'm proud to have been in his band and honoured to be his friend, and I've never tired of his tales from the rock n' roll coalface.

It will come as a surprise to some, but there are some good guys in the music business, and JV is a prince among them.

John Gordon, bassist, Alan Price, Bill Haley & His Comets, Bernie Marsden

John Verity is one of the most indestructible, talented musicians I have ever known. As a singer, guitarist, and expert in studio technology he is untouchable.

I first met him in the early seventies when he joined Rod Argent's group Argent as lead singer. Ever since, I always need him to sing, play and help on my new song demo recordings — often in one of his several own-built excellent studios.

I consider him the perfect example of all that is great about British musicianship. I have been to see him in concert many times. But, until I read this book, I didn't realise how much he has done and how many great musicians he has worked with around the world.

You have to read this book... all those stories are in here.

But also... I do warn you, don't ask him to show you, (as he has done for several famous artists working for me in his studios before), his famous illustrating performance of 'Man, Woman Bulldog'!"

Chris White, producer, songwriter, bassist, The Zombies

Johnny Vee came into my life when his band supported Argent on a UK tour in 1974. This was at a time when, (whether they liked it or not) our support bands dressing room was always full of at least two giant Leslie rotating speakers in mahogany cabinets. These were of course attached to Rod Argent's Hammond organ.

The tour was close to being Russ Ballard's swansong, so JV was in a pretty good position to catch everybody's attention and make himself ready to take over from him.

So, JV joined Argent and the transition was seamless. Before long we set off around the World "looking for adventure, or whatever came our way."

We toured the whole of the civilised world as Argent but eventually we called a halt and decided to take a sabbatical. This was in 1976 when it was time to put our feet up and take stock of the situation.

We decided our brand of progressive rock could easily become heavier and Phoenix was the result. In my humble opinion we were the first power trio. The only small snag was the audience wanted to hear the Argent tunes and on a Phoenix gig in Sheffield we heard a Broad Yorkshire voice cry out: "Play summat we know!"

John's been successfully doing exactly that ever since.

Enjoy the book...

Or we'll put Leslie speakers in your dressing room! (Only joking)

Bob Henrit, drummer, Adam Faith, Argent, The Kinks

Preface

I guess storytelling must be in my DNA, and it comes out as songs sometimes, and sometimes like a nervous 'twitch'.

It must have driven my fellow musicians nuts over the years as 'showtime' approached, because I would get more and more nervous and begin talking incessantly, probably repeating stories I'd told thousands of times before, until it was time to take the stage one more time.

My pre-show stories would be about things that had happened to me or the bands I'd been in, or things that I had witnessed whilst on the road over all these, sixty years of my time in groups/bands, never about my personal life.

People have said to me, "You should write a book" so many times over the years but I never really took the idea seriously until recently.

When Covid-19 and the Lockdown struck in 2020, like many in the *Music World* I searched for ways of keeping in touch with those interested in my music and turned to social media and the Internet for a solution.

In the end I decided to form a *private group* online and deliver weekly live streams to those who would come on board.

Those who came onboard became an amazing group of people, supporting each other through this difficult period, soon becoming a group of friends who really cared.

Each week I would sit in my studio with my group on-line as I told stories and played music for them, and pretty soon one or the other would be repeating the phrase "you should write a book John", or "Why don't you write a book?"

I would usually say, "I'll think about it", but I don't really think I was serious about doing it until after the *Lockdown,* when I started doing shows with my friend Del Bromham, who had recently finished his own autobiography.

Del kept insisting that I should write my story, and the more I thought about it, the more it seemed the right thing to do.

As I wrote, there were periods of my life where the memories were vague, but I was lucky to able to turn to friends who could remind me of the details.

Harvey Rose was the bassist in Tunnel, the band that I first went to America with in the late sixties; Mark Troisi was bassist in the very first John Verity Band, formed in the USA, and Geoff Lyth played guitar with me when I came back to the UK in the early 1970s.

Each of these friends had kept diaries or notes and were able to help me with important details that had slipped my mind, making this memoir as complete as possible…

So here it is, my life, warts, and all, mostly about my music career although of course I have had to open my heart and admit to the many mistakes in my personal life.

It's story of dreams, ups and downs, successes and failures and a man's obsession with all things musical. Join me on my journey…

As I write, it's been over sixty years since I set off on my musical journey. I have no way of knowing if people will be interested, but here goes…

1
Sellars Fold

I was born on the 3rd of July 1949 in St Luke's Hospital, Bradford, West Yorkshire, the first child of Ben and Lilian Verity.

At the time they lived in a one-room apartment (bedsit) in the Manningham area of Bradford but were soon to move to a house in the Great Horton area of the city — 38 Sellars Fold.

There seemed to be everything you needed within a short walking distance, all focused around the main, Great Horton Road, which ran from Bradford town centre directly out toward Queensbury, and eventually Halifax.

From Sellars Fold, across the pedestrian crossing on Great Horton Road onto to Cross Lane, you would find yourself passing the library on your right, the Plaza Picture House on your left, then Great Horton Secondary Modern School, Junior School, Infants School, and finally the Children's Nursery on your right. Next on the left you would see the 'Wreck' (Recreation Area) which was open ground where kids would play football, and once a year the fairground would come.

Directly behind the Wreck was Horton Park, and eventually Park Avenue Sports Ground, which was used for cricket, football and both codes of rugby.

This 37,000-capacity ground was the home of Bradford Park Avenue Football Club for sixty-six years from 1907.

The Park had a lake which usually froze over in the winter. In those days kids were often allowed to 'play out' for most of the day and one winter day I strayed a bit too far into the park. There was a group of older lads on the ice. They tempted me to play a game that resulted in me falling through the ice into the water. I managed to get out and run home crying, to be greeted by a massive bollocking, and slapped legs from Mum!

38 Sellars Fold was a 'one up, one down/back-to-back' home with

just one room upstairs and one room downstairs — plus of course the cellar, which is where the coal was stored.
There was no bathroom or toilet inside the house.

My brother Paul and I shared a bed behind a curtain in the bedroom at first, until dad built a partition to give us all some privacy.

I remember our bed had a blue and white bottom sheet, and Paul and I knew exactly how may stripes determined the dividing line between his side and mine.
Woe betide anyone straying over that line!

There was a small metal hatch at the bottom of the outside wall beneath the window for the Coalman to empty the sacks of coal through so that it landed in the cellar.

Each house in Sellars Fold had three neighbours, one at each side and one at the back and I remember you could bang on any one of the three internal walls to alert a neighbour to come round for a cuppa!

The door to the cellar steps was in the corner of the room and as you opened the door you would find the kitchen sink, with its one cold water tap.

The Gas Meter was under this sink (more of this later).

Number 38 was in a row of houses that faced directly on to the street and a similar row at the back had a stone yard area where there were outbuildings, or 'middins' as we used to call them.

This is where each house in the street had a toilet, and space for the dustbin to be kept. I guess our toilet was about one hundred yards from the house. I still remember the nail behind the toilet door on which was impaled squares of newspaper on which to wipe your bum!

I spent a lot of my early life with Mum, as brother Paul didn't arrive until I was five years old.

My memories of these times are sketchy, but I do remember pomegranates, eaten with a pin, I suspect to keep me quiet for a while as I tried to eat each seed, one at a time with the pin. I also remember Mayday, when each year I would dress up my three-wheeler bike with coloured crepe paper and wait at the end of the street for the procession heading down Great Horton Road toward the town centre.

I would be allowed to join the procession for a while, pedalling along with the other kids on their dressed-up bikes until it was time to turn around and head for home.

Dad used to give me my pocket money once a week, pointing to the 'money box' under the sink and I would obediently push my coins into the slot, turning the key until they dropped.

It wasn't until years later that I realised that the 'money box' was actually the gas meter! I would receive my real pocket money later in the week, thinking it was a 'second instalment'.

There was no electricity at first, I remember being allowed to walk to the corner shop at the end of the street when I was small, to buy the Gas Mantles for the lights in the house, and to buy *Players* or *Senior Service* cigarettes for Mum and Dad — I don't suppose a toddler would be allowed to do this now!

There was a large black cast iron range with the coal fire and an oven, although I think we had a gas oven as well.

Once a week Dad would get the big, galvanised bath from where it was hanging behind the cellar door, place it in front of the fire and fill it with pans of hot water, heated on the cooker in a big pan.
Paul and I would get in first (more of Paul later), followed by Dad and then finally Mum after Paul and I were sent to bed. Dad would drag the bath out of the door and empty it into the street, as did everyone in Sellars Fold.

Eventually, electricity was supplied to the houses, but only for the lighting, although pretty soon people were running electric fires from the light sockets — it can't have been very safe!

Times must have been hard, I remember having to answer the door, when I was quite small, to tell the Rent Man that Mum and Dad were out.

Mum would be hiding behind the setee…

Mum had two sisters, Aunty Vi, and Aunty Freddie. (Yes, that's right Aunty Fred!) — but of course it must have been Frederika although I never heard anyone say that.

I never met my Grandparents on Mum's side as they both died quite young. They worked in Vaudeville, and Mum went to different schools for a while as they travelled from theatre to theatre across the country entertaining.

I think they settled for a short while in County Durham, which is where Mum and the girls were born.

I'm a Yorkshire Geordie!

Dad's Mum and Dad Fred and Eleanor lived in Wakefield and although I do remember visiting, I guess we weren't a particularly close-knit family as I don't have any real memories of these visits, although I only ever heard grandma referred to as 'Nellie'.

Of my cousins I really only remember Chris (Christine), Alma, and Arthur. They were all in Wakefield, as were my grandparents, about fifteen miles from Bradford.

Dads' family were coal miners, the boys were all born in Ingleton, North Yorkshire where there was a pit. They will have all been expected to go down the pit when they were old enough although one of Dad's brothers Reg went on to be a pharmacist.

I don't think Dad ever went down the pit although he did work there, mostly topside as he had an ace card up his sleeve!

Many of the pits has a brass band and Dad discovered that if you were a talented player, you would receive preferential treatment. Brass bands were important in those days and Dad became a proficient Cornet player, good enough to be in the band. Consequently, much of his time at work was spent practicing with the band, or sitting in a shed, smoking, and talking about it instead of going down the pit. Perfect!

Ingleton was a small pit and eventually it became unviable and was closed.

The mining community had to find work elsewhere so the Verity's moved south to Durkar, in South Yorkshire near Wakefield.

There was a pumping station for the coal mine at nearby Crigglestone and I believe all the boys found work there.

Dad joined the Crigglestone Brass Band, a band that was already successful in the brass band world and seemed to settle well in the new location.

Meanwhile, Mum had previously been married and had a daughter, Ella (Ellen) just before war broke out in 1939. Mum had begun training as a nurse and was sent to London to help with the war effort, leaving Ella behind to be looked after by family as it wasn't safe for children in London.

Mum had two jobs in London — one was nursing, the other was building bombs!

Mum's husband was in the British Army and was sadly killed in 1942 whilst fighting in Egypt.

She continued her work in London, returning to the Northeast after the war, hoping to collect Ella and start a new life.

On returning to the Northeast Mum admitted to family that she was in a new relationship.

They were so angry with her that she was sent packing without Ella and told never to return.

To her great regret, Mum did as she was told, and lost touch with Ella until many years later (more on this in a bit).

This Rock 'n' Roll Won't Last You Know!

2
On The Move

I never did know how Mum and Dad met, but by the time I came along they were living in Bradford.

Dad was working at the roller-skating rink in Bradford and Mum was working sometimes as a barmaid and sometimes as bookkeeper.

Dad's job seemed to involve coaching skaters and general stuff around the place. A bit of Jack-of-all-trades, I guess.

The Rink burned down and was replaced by the local 'Mecca' on the same site. The flat roof of the Rink was coated in tar, and apparently Dad was on the roof repairing it on the day the fire took hold and destroyed the place.

He seemed to change jobs quite a lot, I think he preferred driving to being stuck in one place. By the time he took a job with local soft drink company Horton Direct I was old enough to tag along as he made deliveries. Pretty soon I was helping, and by the time I was about nine years old I was working weekends in the factory, on the machine that washed and sterilised the bottles. The water was close to boiling, there's no way it would be allowed these days!

Mum was the perfect barmaid with an hourglass figure — apparently once when I was very small, I was watching her get ready for work putting her makeup on.

Dad said I was looking at her a bit disapprovingly as she had a low-cut top on showing lots of cleavage.

She noticed, turned, and said to me "it's alright love I'm starting a new job tonight, so it'll be all eyes on deck". Priceless!

One of my friends around this time was Ian Scollick, who lived next door in Sellars Fold. His big brother Peter was a teenager and we used to go with him sometimes when he visited his girlfriend, Angela Racher. I remember Angela's name because I was in love!

Angela's Mum and Dad didn't mind having a houseful, and there was always music on the record player.

I guess this was when it got into my blood. The raw sound of early Elvis records and all the other stuff from the time, it must have been about 1957.

I soon wanted, no, *needed* a guitar.

Around this time the rumours that Sellars Fold might be demolished were growing so it was time to find somewhere new. I was trying to persuade my parents to get me a guitar and just before we left Sellars Fold for good I got my very first one — a virtually unplayable Spanish acoustic. I discovered in later years it was just like the same one a million other budding guitarists had.

So, we left Sellars Fold and at first lived in a one-room bedsit, again in Manningham, where I had first started life. It was pretty spartan as you can guess — at night I used to spot rats running across the furniture piled in front of the bay window waiting for a new home.

If Dad saw them, he'd open the door to the lobby and shout 'Baron!'

The white, albino Alsatian belonging to neighbours on the top floor used to run down and hunt for the rat, taking it outside once he caught it. I loved Baron.

I can't remember how long we were in Manningham, but next stop was a 'Semi' in Wrose, a nice area on the outskirts of Bradford, close to Shipley and Saltaire. We weren't there for long, I think Mum and Dad were struggling financially and had overstretched themselves to get the house.

We had a lodger for a while, a nice Greek Cypriot guy called Nicodemus but even that wasn't enough, and our next destination was back in Great Horton not far from Sellars Fold.

Daisy Street was rows of back-to-back houses again and this time we lived around the back.

Number 36 Daisy Street was down a passage from the street, slightly bigger than Sellars Fold but brother Paul and I were still in the same bed.

A neighbour, Mr Smith kept pigeons and after a while he helped me to build a pigeon loft and gave me some birds to start with. I loved my feathered friends and after a while had quite a few.

Once trained I could let them out knowing they would all come home safely at the end of the day, and I at first I was planning to follow Mr Smith and enter my best birds into races like he did, but I'd already caught another bug that was taking away my interest in pigeons for good...

Mum seemed to have reverted to her childhood insecurities, finding it hard to settle. A few months after moving into 36 Daisy Street I came home from school to find the house empty.

Nobody locked their doors back then, so on getting home from school I simply went to open the door, only to find it locked.
I looked through the window and all the furniture had gone, but before I could get really upset, I heard Mum's voice — coming from next door. They had moved to 38 Daisy Street!

Mum said there was less damp than in 36...

I was still struggling with the Spanish guitar, although I had managed to 'electrify' it by sellotaping a contact mic to the front soundboard and plugging it into the 'Gram' input of our radio.

There was an Army Surplus Store in Bradford, one of my favourite places, where you could buy all sorts of electrical, ex-army suff. It was like Aladdin's Cave.

The contact mic I had found was actually a British Army Tank Gunner's throat mic. Perfect for a guitar pickup!

By now I was studying (not) at Grange Boys Grammar School.

I was finding it hard, as there's not a lot of point studying at Grammar School when you're destined to be a rich famous Pop Star is there?

Anyway, the good news was that we were about to move again, this time a little further out of town to 853 Great Horton Road.

Why the good news? For the first time, I was getting my own bedroom.

The attic bedroom was amazing, I had my own window looking out onto the alley below. 853 was at the end of the row so I'm guessing the attic bedrooms in the other houses didn't have a window. Luxury!

I was in my own little world up there, by now I'd taken ownership of that old radio which was now my guitar amp.

For further entertainment I wanted to listen to Radio Luxemburg, so back down to Army Surplus to get the parts to build my own crystal set, with headphones — again from a tank.
Reception wasn't great until I got a really long piece of wire for an aerial, dangled out of the bedroom window.

I still wasn't 100% satisfied so I tied something (I think it was an old plimsole) to the end of the aerial wire and threw it out high into the air over Great Horton Road so that it hung over the wires running down the middle of the road.

Perfect! Radio Luxemburg was loud and clear, although there was still the 'phasing' that we had all grown accustomed to as the signal drifted in and out.

Pretty good though.

That was until there was a knock on the door from the telephone engineers enquiring whose wire it was running over the telephone wire running down the street.

Apparently, the neighbours weren't very happy at having to listen to Radio Luxemburg coming down their phone when they were trying to make a call! Oops.

So, I had to find a new location for my aerial. No harm done.

3
The Plan

I had noticed an advert for *Vox* guitars and amplifiers in one of the papers. It seemed you could buy one by mail order. I was trying to buck up courage to discuss it with Mum and Dad — after all a budding Rock 'n' Roll star needs a proper guitar, right?

Anyway, I knew money was tight at home. But I had my paper round...

So, I sent for the catalogue and when it arrived, I fell in love with the *Vox* Clubman II.

I had to have one, in white. It was 21 guineas.

I knew there was no chance of getting Mum and Dad to agree to paying for it so I had to go it alone. In the catalogue, there was a hire purchase agreement, so I filled it in and signed 'Ben Verity'. Off to the post box and wait...

Every morning I would set off for school, get about fifty yards down the road where there was a wall to hide behind and wait for Mum and Dad to go to work.

Once they'd gone, I'd go back home and wait.

Eventually the box arrived, I hid it in my bedroom and started to go to school again.

This was heaven, every night I would get the guitar out, plug it into the 'Gram' input in the back of the radio and practice. No-one seemed to notice the difference in sound. Until...

I came home from school and Mum was sitting there looking a bit irritated.

"Where's the guitar John?"

"What guitar Mum?"

Then she waved a letter at me. The letter congratulating Ben Verity on his purchase of a white *Vox* Clubman II electric guitar...

So... I'd been rumbled. Dad pretended to be furious, but I think that really, he liked the idea of me going out and playing the clubs — with his personal manager Ben Verity!

Once the initial shock had died down, I was given an ultimatum. I had to learn some songs and earn the money to pay for the guitar. My paper round wasn't enough to cover the 19/11 a month for the payments (19 shillings and eleven pence).
So, there I was, furiously practising in my room as Mum and Dad got to finding some bookings for me — 'Johnny Vee'.

I had another shock, a massive, life changing shock in store for my parents soon but more of that later.

Back to my bedroom to get a repertoire of four songs together, as the Working Men's Club dates were on the horizon, and I really wasn't ready.

I soon got a chance to try things out. Dad had booked a short holiday to Butlins Holiday Camp and had fixed up for me to enter the talent competition.

I was horrified, but of course went along with it and after my rendition of 'If I Had A Hammer' was awarded Third Prize. Not exactly number one *Top of the Pops* but it was a start.

When we got home there was a package for Dad. Turns out it was from the printer's shop, Dad's business cards "Ben Verity, Personal Manager of Johnny Vee'. Oh good grief!

After Dad passed away, I found one of these cards amongst his stuff.

Next job was to get a proper amplifier, and now that Dad was properly involved, and I had a couple of dates in the diary I was able to get one on credit.

We went to Bryon's Harmony House, a music shop in Bradford to get some advice and look at some amps and came away with a *Watkins Clubman*, (and a weekly payment card).
My first proper Amp!

Charlie Watkins was one of the first UK guitar amp builders and was soon to change the name to WEM.

WEM became one of the earliest companies to build proper modular PA systems with a mixer separate from the power amp, meaning that you could connect multiple power amps to build a really big PA system.

My little Clubman amp was only about five watts though, probably not as loud as the average TV set these days.

The dates I had were on Sunday lunchtimes, when I often had a short spot in between a soprano singer and a stripper! My introduction to the glamorous life of Showbiz.

I was embarrassed about this, but luckily the venues were in Wakefield and surrounding pit villages so no one in Bradford knew anything about it.

What I really wanted was to be in a group, so I set about trying to find people to play with (musically of course!)

Our local paper, the *Bradford Telegraph and Argus* had an entertainments section with ads for musicians, and Bryon's had little cards in the window from groups searching for players.

By 1963 I was in The Chillas and practising regularly at a church hall on St Mary's Road, Bradford.

We used to travel to gigs in a butcher's van as we were all too young to drive.

We played mostly pubs and clubs, but our best gig by miles was one Saturday afternoon at the Towers Hall Cinema playing in the interval.

I can't remember how or what we played — but will always remember the other group who played that day.

Dave Arran and the Crusaders had *Vox* amps on chrome stands, the two guitarists had real *Fender Stratocasters*, and the bassist a real *Fender Precision Bass*! I was in heaven just looking at them.

My other most striking recollection was the girls screaming at us as we played!

The only other time I'd seen a Strat in the flesh was the day I took the bus to Leeds because I'd heard that there was one in the window of Bradley's Music there.

I stood on the pavement outside the shop looking through the window at this amazing thing from Outer Space. I had to have one, and in the end I did.

Incidentally, the rhythm guitarist in The Crusaders was a guy called Cliff Dutton, a real music legend in Bradford. I wasn't to know at the time, but our paths would soon cross again when I had a bit more experience under my belt.

So, things were progressing steadily now, I was a regular customer at Bryon's and had stepped up to a better guitar and amp, added to that payment card. I was now the proud owner of a red *Hofner Colorama* guitar and a *WEM Control ER15 (Pick-A-Back)* amp.

Around this time, I remember chatting to another young guitar player outside Bryon's. He like me, had been in to buy some strings and as we chatted, he invited me to come to his house to swap ideas. His name was Allan and he lived with his grandparents, not far from me in Bradford.

Allan was a bit older than me, and I thought I might learn something, so we arranged for me to call and see him at his house.

I was in for a huge shock! His playing was unbelievable, and once he had started, I didn't dare get my guitar out and play. His full name was Allan Holdsworth — soon to become one of the most revered players on the jazz circuit, although he always refused to be pigeonholed.

Allan was simply the best I had ever seen.

I did eventually pluck up the courage to get my guitar out, and Allan showed me some lovely chord inversions that I use to this day.

Sadly, Allan died in 2017.

Now I was getting ready to move up a gear…

Moving Up — And Out…

For a while I was happy to jump from group to group, honing my skills despite some pretty heavyweight personal stuff going on in my life.

I'm not going to get into lots of detail, but my girlfriend Joan was pregnant!

Ian was born on 8th May 1964 — I was still fourteen years old.

Mum completely freaked out when I came home from school one day and told her I might need more spending money to help with the baby!

This began a chain of events that changed everything.

Mum and Dad decided to move us all to Wakefield to make a fresh start.

Looking back, of course I feel terrible about abandoning Joan and Ian, but they were safe in a loving family, and I was far too young to take on the responsibility…

Ian and I are great friends now thankfully – more about how we came to get together later…

So, I left Grange Boys Grammar School early, and never went to school in Wakefield.

First of all I got a Saturday job which became a full-time job at K Shoes in the town centre, but my first loves were music and electronics.

Pretty soon I found my way into electronics when I began an apprenticeship at Lodge Radio and TV. I was allowed at first to replace the broken thermostats in irons (yes, we actually used to fix things in those days!) and climb onto high roofs to fit TV aeriels.

I hated the TV aeriel bit, but I also hated the way apprentices were treated. Apprentices get really tired of being sent to the wholesalers to collect things like a left-handed screwdriver, a glass hammer, or a long stand!

One real positive however was that one of the other blokes working there was a bass player and Tony Cockell and I formed a duo – John and Tony (original!).

We put together a set and began playing the working men's clubs in the Wakefield area but before we got really established something else turned up.

My chance to become a full-time musician!

One lunchtime at Lodges I was reading the *Yorkshire Post* and skimming through the jobs section. To my surprise there was an advert by a local Brewery for musicians and a place to go for an audition. Without telling anyone I skipped work and went to do the audition.

Following that day with Allan I had become obsessed with learning chords. Allan had said that if you knew all the chords on the guitar, and their inversions it would really help when it came to improvising and working with other musicians.

I quickly bought a book (from Bryon's of course!) that had 500 chords and inversions in it and learned every one.

It turned out that I was actually auditioning for a jazz combo, and my knowledge of chords got me the job. I was a professional musician!

The pay from the brewery was better than my apprentices pay at Lodge Electrical, and soon I was ready to improve my equipment again – with the help of Dad.

Dad drove me to Leeds, and as we entered Bradleys Music what did I see hanging on the wall? A second-hand, but mint condition Fender Stratocaster in Daphne blue for 120 guineas.

The Strat, plus a brand-new Selmer Zodiac 50 amp cost a lot of money but Dad was guarantor on the credit agreement, and I finally had the proper tools for a "Pro".

This Rock 'n' Roll Won't Last You Know!

4
Best Laid Plans...

The Brewery had a plan. They had closed and totally refitted several of their larger pubs, with a plan to make them cater for a *better class* of customer. Our job was to provide smooth jazz music in the background to add to the atmosphere. The venue we were assigned to, the Fforde Green in Leeds had been quite a rough pub in the past I think, but this new format was going to change all that.

But of course, it didn't.

Try as we might, we couldn't create the calm atmosphere we were supposed to be providing, and the fights would still kick off as they had before. It was chaos!

The only time we managed to get the audiences' attention was at the end of the evening when I began perfecting what was to become a bit of a trademark – making a terrible racket with my guitar!

Our Organist, Norman, would start by playing the theme from *The Dam Busters* and this seemed to grab everyone's attention. We would play the whole thing, then I would turn my guitar and amp up to full volume and, using the Strat's tremolo arm, make the sound of airplanes diving.

The Selmer Zodiac amp had a spring reverb, and I would kick the amp as the notes dived from my guitar making a loud crashing sound a bit like explosions. The crowd used to go nuts — but Dad also used to get a bit concerned about the condition of the amp we were still paying for. "It looks like someone's been kicking it, lad"!

The Brewery's masterplan just didn't work, and before long the project was shelved, and we were out of work.

Back at Mum and Dad's house, 1 John Street, Wakefield I was thinking I'd really screwed things up. No job, a payment card from Bryon's and a Hire Purchase agreement for the Strat and Selmer amp. Then the phone rang – Norman had a new residency for us at a Working

Men's Club near Leeds. Phew!!

Swillington Miners Welfare didn't sound very glamorous, but it was a gig. A residency in fact meaning we were tied to it and couldn't do any other work for as long as we were playing there.

I used to leave my amp there — by now I had become the proud owner of a Selmer Thunderbird 100watt combo amp. It was huge and had four 12-inch speakers and a chrome stand with wheels. Dad signed the hire purchase agreement once again and drove me there to collect it, this time from *Kitchens* in Leeds.

100 watts was totally unnecessary in a working men's club of course but I was a budding rock star, and 100 watts was part of the outfit.

As with my previous amp, the Thunderbird had a spring reverb so I could continue my practice of kicking the amp to get the sound of explosions as we played *The Dam Busters*.

I don't know if it was due to this treatment, but the Thunderbird proved to be unreliable — I lost count of the number of times we wheeled it across the shop floor at *Kitchens* to complain that it had gone wrong again.

As I said, I used to leave the amp at the club, and I had got myself a Vespa Sportique motor scooter.

With this newfound bit of independence, I decided to do bit of detective work during a break from the club. As a child I had picked up small bits of information related to my half-sister Ella. I had heard a place called Wheatley Hill mentioned, and Peterlee, both in the Northeast, in County Durham.

So, off up the Great North Road to try to find Ella in the hope that she and Mum could be reunited somehow. My plan initially was to go to the Doctor's Surgery in Peterlee to see if they had any knowledge of the family, hoping I might get an address.

I believed that Ella's Surname was Lee, and the receptionist confirmed that she had been a patient but was no longer in the area.

So off to Peterlee, where I had more success. The receptionist there gave me an address when I explained my predicament, and I set off to the house in question.

I still remember the feeling I had as I stood on the doorstep, tapping on the door. I had written Mum's contact details on a piece of paper that I held in my hand, shaking as I stood waiting for an answer.

The door opened and a young girl stood before me. I knew right away that it was Ella, don't ask me how, it was just a feeling. I could see past her into the room where an older lady was sitting in a chair watching us as I quickly explained who I was, passing the little piece of paper to Ella.

I wasn't invited in, Ella looked uncomfortable and now the old lady looked angry as I stood there not knowing what to do. There was an awkward silence, so I said goodbye, turned and walked away to my scooter and rode off.

The ride home was strange, I didn't know if I'd done the right thing or not but there was the satisfaction that at least I'd tried…

So, back to business.

I would ride to the club on my scooter, with my beloved Strat in its case resting across the footrest, sticking out left and right. I was an accident waiting to happen, and it did.

On my way to the club one evening an oncoming car was signalling to turn left. Fine, except he turned right, in front of me. I hit the car at speed, launched myself into the air and landed flat on my back in a pub carpark. The Strat followed me, but by a more direct route, sliding along the ground behind me.

The driver of the car ran over to me, and I couldn't feel anything, my body was just numb. He looked so upset that I muttered, "it's alright mate, it was my fault".

Police and ambulance came, and of course when it came to Court my admission of guilt was used against me, my license was endorsed, and I was fined for 'driving without due care and attention".

On the day of the accident, I was delivered home to John Street in an ambulance, and obviously Mum was upset, but Dad just called me a bloody idiot which was a typical response from him.

It took a few days for me to get back on my feet and during this time a surprise came in the post.

Mum received a letter from Ella, finally getting them together after all those years. They remained close until mum passed away in 1981.

I've kept in touch with Ella's daughters, Jill and Catherine. Jill lives in Arundel, West Sussex with her family and Catherine has settled in Bristol with hers, although sadly we don't get many opportunities to meet up, other than when I happen to be gigging near them.

This Rock 'n' Roll Won't Last You Know!

5
Back To Bradford

Time for a change in more ways than one. I wasn't playing the kind of music I really wanted to play, although I was grateful for the chance to turn professional with the trio.

The scooter was in a bad way, so I needed a new mode of transport, and I needed a better amplifier! The Selmer was proving to be really unreliable, and I lost count of the amount of times Dad had to take me back to shop with it, to have it repaired.

Eventually I settled on a Marshall 100 with 2 4x12 speaker cabinets — a Marshall Stack!

With my new rig, I wanted to move back to Bradford, where the music scene was healthier for an up-and-coming Rock Star!

First things first, I had to have transport to give me independence.

I only had a license to drive a motorcycle, but I was allowed to drive a three-wheeler, with L-plates on.

I found a second-hand dark blue Trojan three-wheeler for the princely sum of £25.00, it had two wheels at the front and one at the back and sounded a bit like a motorbike. No room for an amp but I could get my guitar in it okay.

I found a bedsit in Bradford, fibbing about my age and went about trying to find a band, although nothing I first got involved with really suited me.

I had come along musically quite a bit, and my expectations were a lot higher now. I took a job at *Sunwin House* in Bradford working as a window-dresser. I'd flirted with window dressing when I worked at *K Shoes* in Wakefield, and I guess because it's creative I liked it quite a lot.

It brought some money in, and it gave me a chance to meet like-minded people again in Bradford. I kept an eye on the local papers and before long it appeared — "Guitarist wanted for group with record contract".

I auditioned for *Allen Pounds Get Rich* and got the job!

It was early 1967 and I was in a band with a record deal. They already had a single out on Parlophone Records, dates in the diary and a van with lipstick writing all over it proclaiming undying love for the guys in the band.

At the end of our first rehearsal, I was given a copy of the single and told to learn the A-side 'Searching In The Wilderness' for the next rehearsal. Just as I was leaving, I was casually told "oh and learn the B-side as well".

Back at the bedsit I got the A-side done in no time, a piece of cake. The flip side seemed equally easy until it came to the guitar solo — it was unplayable, or at least it was for me. I was sunk, sure I'd lose the job as their music was beyond my reach...

The day came to get to the rehearsal with my heart in my boots, my dreams of being in a recording band were on the rocks.

I had decided to be up-front about it and admitted right away that there was no way I could play the B-side. The guys broke into fits of laughter, they were just winding me up. It turns out that the guy I was replacing in the band was Allan Holdsworth — he of the long fingers and blistering guitar technique.

So, here I was, living the dream or so I thought, although the dream was to be short lived.

Allen Pound (Marston) and Trevor (McPartland) the drummer were the only original members of the band that had played on the record, as me and bassist Mick Jackson were new recruits.

I soon discovered why, as it became obvious that Allen was basically a PR guy/salesman trying to make a quick buck in the music biz. Definitely not a singer...

We did make some unforgettable recordings that remained unreleased but the whole thing was pretty shallow to be honest. Nothing seemed to get paid for, and I'm sure the lipstick writing on the van was done by Allen and his partner!

The only thing I got out of it was a new hairstyle — the first thing they did was to chop off my beautiful quiff and bring me up to date with a modern crop. I hated it at first, but my Teddy Boy look was gone forever.

The Legend – Cliff Dutton!

Cliff Dutton, he of Dave Arran and The Crusaders, the group I watched in awe a few years ago at the Towers Hall Cinema show when I was still learning my craft.

Cliff was an important part of the music scene in Bradford, he was always there with a band in some shape or form.

There were several things important to a budding band member in those days, perhaps more important than musical ability in some cases.

Cliff had been in some important groups / bands on the local music circuit. He was a competent guitar player you might say, but more than this he had a van, a PA system, and the ability to arrange gigs. He was a good organiser and could fix stuff too. What more did you need?

I can't remember how it happened, but my next stop in 1967 was Cliff's current group The Collection. Once again, I was replacing Allan Holdsworth, massive shoes to step into. We were gigging up and down the country, and a friend of Cliff's was trying to resurrect my still shattered Vespa Sportique. The Trojan was proving far too dangerous, with a mind of its own it would suddenly change direction for no apparent reason leading to far too many near-misses.

The Vespa was proving to be too difficult to fix, and anyway my equipment was getting bigger — the Thunderbird that had just proved too unreliable was gone and the new kid on the block – *Marshall 100* with its two big speaker cabinets needed more room.

The bottom speaker cabinet was a tall 4x12 with another, but bevelled 4x12 on top and finally the 100-watt head on the very top. I still had my Strat, a Tone Bender pedal and a Wah-Wah pedal. Ready to rock!

My new form of transport was a British Racing Green Austin A35 van with just enough room for my kit.

The van was great except for a bit of rust in the sills under the doors — soon rectified by our trusty Cliff Dutton, who covered the rusty evidence with bent steel, sprayed the correct colour. Good as new (ish).

Cliff was trying to arrange some new gigs in Germany, but the scene had changed over there. Seems you had to have a lady in the band so in came Brenda Martine to make us Brenda And The Collection. Brenda was an excellent vocalist and fitted in right away alongside me on lead guitar, Cliff on rhythm, Pete Spencer on drums and Don Maundrill on bass.

Around this time my favourite album was the Bluesbreakers 'Beano' album with Eric Clapton playing a Gibson Les Paul and that had started my longing for a Gibson. I still had my Strat, but also a Gibson-like *Grimshaw* guitar, made in the UK. It wasn't a real Gibson though and imagine my surprise when the guitarist in the other band playing at a gig, we were doing took a liking to the *Grimshaw*.

He asked me if I was interested in selling or trading it and I asked him what he had to trade. He opened a case on the floor and there was a Gibson! It was a Les Paul Special double cutaway, in really bad shape but it was a Gibson, nevertheless.

The original Les Paul was a single cutaway guitar, but sales were flagging so in 1959 they untroduced a double cutaway model in the hope that a more modern shape would pick up sales. It was initially introduced as a student guitar in two versions, the Special, and the Junior. They also did 'TV' versions in white.

Gibson weren't to know that with the rise of players like Clapton, Peter Green, Mick Taylor, and Paul Butterfield in the US the popularity of the old-style Les Paul would suddenly peak. This iconic version ceased production in 1961.

The guitar I was being offered was a mess. The neck had been broken off where it joined the body and repaired with metal plate screwed in place. It had also been hand-painted orange! I plugged it into my amp, fired it up and fell in love. It was a beast!

So, the deal was done, I had a Gibson. I had an ideal setup really, Marshall amp with both Fender and Gibson guitars.

They say all good things come to an end... We were playing a gig in Hull sometime later, when a guy in the audience just in front of me seemed to be staring. Then he was gone. Then he was back — with two policemen.

We came off stage and the guy and the Police were waiting by the dressing room door. The guy said the Gibson was his and he had a photo of himself with it to prove it. The picture was obviously taken prior to it being repainted and I was sticking my ground.

I, along with the guitar was taken to the police station and put into an interview room. Terrified I sat and waited. By now it was the early hours of the morning, and I was tired and scared.

After a while the coppers came back and started to ask me questions. Where did I get the guitar? Do I have a receipt? Who did I buy it from? Did I have any convictions? I told the story truthfully and insisted the there wasn't sufficient evidence to prove the guitar was the other guys. After a while they left me again, alone.

After what seemed like an age, the Seargent came in, looked me straight in the eye and said, "did you nick it lad?" I said no. He said, "you'd better take it and get off home then".

I was into the A35 and out of Hull in a flash, feeling relieved and lucky. It could have gone either way.

The next few gigs were uneventful, I was enjoying my time in The Collection then we were doing a gig at Bingley Nurses College — an outdoor event when a change would come.

There were other bands on the bill and after we'd played, a couple of guys from one of the other bands came up to me asking for a chat. They said would I meet them later and pointed to their van, a long wheelbase transit with windows and aircraft seats. Clearly, they were a cut above us in our Commer J4.

The Ford Transit revolutionised band travel in the sixties. They were perfect with enough room to get everyone in seated, with a partition at the back separating the gear instead of everyone crammed on top of each other and the gear as was usually the case. Perfect.

So, I met them as planned and they offered me a job. I was fully professional with Cliff, earning a set wage. They offered me more, and of course I get to ride in the Transit. Oh and they had a roadie to do the driving and the gear!

I explained to Cliff, and he was fine about it, pleased for me improving my chances.

So I was the new member of The Richard Kent Style, a 6-piece band with brass section known mostly as a soul band although that was about to change.

This Rock 'n' Roll Won´t Last You Know!

6
New Horizons 1968

The Richard Kent Style was based in Manchester, which was a small complication but not a deal breaker.

I would travel to Manchester to rehearse with the understanding that my first gig would be when the band began an engagement at The Casino, Estoril, Portugal. I had never been that far from home!

The rehearsals were great, and Al, (drummer) and Harvey, (bassist) were a cracking rhythm section. It was the first time I'd played with a brass section, and I loved it.

The band was tight and Harvey (Starr), the lead singer doubled on valve trombone to complete the 3-piece brass section. Al Powell, Harvey Rose and myself soon gelled into a tight unit and every gig was a pleasure as time went on, but first of all I had a bit of a shock to contend with.

I think I stayed at Al's parents house on the night before we were due to travel to Portugal.
The van was due to come round and pick everyone up in turn, and once Al and I had got in we went and picked up everyone else, or so I thought. Everyone was in the van, but we stopped again, and to my shock and surprise the old guitarist got in! I don't think he had been told either and there was a stunned silence as we headed south.

It seemed that the guy I had replaced in the band didn't know anything about it. We never discussed it, so I don't know the details, but we all went to Portugal and Neil, and I took it in turn to play the guitar parts and then he disappeared once we got back to Manchester. Strange.

The trip to Portugal was eventful. I didn't get to travel in the Transit with the aircraft seats, it was booked into the garage for repairs so our Agency, Kennedy Street arranged for us to borrow a van from one of their other bands. A transit, but without the trimmings.

So off we went, heading for Southampton, running a bit late, so with a fully loaded van we were really going for it and daren't stop despite the van starting to make a terrible noise at the front.

We made it in time for the ferry and were shocked to find that the front wheel nuts hadn't be tightened fully — we were lucky not to lose a wheel at 90mph!

Southampton to Bilbao in a ship was not my favourite journey, I don't like ships and I don't like throwing up. We made it safely though and Dave, our roadie (also known as The Goblin) made a start on the long drive toward Portugal.

We arrived at the Spanish/Portuguese border safely enough but when they asked for the van documents, we didn't have them. Panic set in, and a frantic phone call to Kennedy Street resulted in arrangements made to send the stuff to us asap while we waited not so patiently at the border, staying in a hotel located conveniently in no man's land between Spain and Portugal....

Finally we were off. The rest of the journey was fairly uneventful, and we arrived safely in Estoril.

The promoter had booked us into a small hotel / *Pensioni* and soon we were at the Casino awaiting our instructions.

We were told we had to play two shows per night, the first one at 9:00pm in the restaurant, which was huge, on the first floor and the second show in the night club which was at the top of the building. We had to set up the equipment and play in the restaurant, then break everything down and get it to the nightclub via staff service corridors and lifts, then set it up again and play. Those were the days!

We had a few weeks of this schedule to look forward to so best to get used to it!

It was 1968, and life was to change quite a bit. This band was much busier than any I'd ever been involved with.

I had moved to Manchester with my first wife Eileen, to a tiny flat on Cheetham Hill Road, close to the town centre. Close enough to walk into town, and handy if I needed any repairs or servicing to my amps.

Graham and Anne Mellor had a shop called A1 Music in town, and he was brilliant with tube/valve amps, perfect...

The Richard Kent Style was well respected, and the work situation was great. When we weren't gigging on our own, we spent a lot of time working as Dave Berry's backing group. Dave had, had several hit records and had a very full diary. These were the days of the cabaret venues and *Theatre Clubs,* and he was very popular on this circuit.

When working with Dave we would do fourteen gigs a week. That would be two different venues each night, with a 9:00pm show at one club followed by a midnight show at the other.

Even now when we travel up and down the country if I see a sign for a town I will immediately think of the town where we used to do the second show. It was called 'Doubling'.

It was hard work I guess, but we breezed through it — we were living the dream of every young musician after all — fourteen gigs a week!

We would drive to the first gig, set the gear up, do the show, break the gear down and pack it into the van and drive to the second gig, unload the van, set the gear up, do the second show and pack the gear again usually ending up at a small hotel or 'Pro Digs'.

Pro Digs were basically small hotels that catered for performers, so no problems arriving late at night or in the early hours and no early breakfasts. Breakfast was served at a much later time allowing the guests a bit of a lie-in after the late night.

We would encounter many of the popular entertainers of the time when staying in Pro Digs, sometimes finding ourselves sharing the breakfast table with a famous comedian, singer, or dancer.

When we were doubling, it would usually be the same two venues for the whole week.

After a while we decided to have two sets of equipment to make it easier. The week would usually start on a Sunday, so we'd go to the first gig, set up one set of gear and do the show, then leave most of the gear behind and get to the midnight show with second set of gear, set that up and do the show.

I don't think we ever had a second drum kit, so that would have been broken down and taken with us between venues but by then I had two amps and Harvey had a second bass rig.

My new acquisition was a Fender Super Reverb combo, the beginning of my love affair with Fender amps. I loved it!

Another change of gear happened almost by accident.

I loved my Gibson Les Paul, but I used to stare at Gibson catalogues and lust after a slightly different model. The new shape Gibson Les Paul Custom, soon to be renamed SG was also known as the 'Fretless Wonder' and was made famous by Sister Rosetta Tharpe

— 'The Godmother of Rock 'n' Roll".

American guitarist Les Paul, who had endorsed the earlier Les Paul models didn't like this new shape and shortly after its introduction insisted on having his name removed from it. Hence the new name SG Custom.

One night we arrived at a gig in Newtown, in the Northwest of England to find that there was another band on the bill as well as us. We were sharing the dressing room, and I walked into the empty dressing to find the other bands stuff in there including a Gibson guitar case. I couldn't resist peeking into the case, and there it was, a Fretless Wonder!

Not only that, but it was also an early example from when they were still called Les Paul, with a nameplate between the bottom of the fretboard and the neck pickup to prove it.

Just then I heard footsteps behind me and someone from the other band appeared. He introduced himself as the guitarist, and said it was okay to look at his guitar, and he asked what guitar did I play? I took my Les Paul from its case and handed it to him. He gazed at my guitar and said, "blimey I've always wanted one of these".

Well, we chatted for a while and eventually decided that each of us would play the other's guitar tonight, and at the end of the night talk about a possible deal if we were both interested. I loved his guitar, and he loved mine, so we agreed to swap.

I went home that night with my dream guitar, one that was to stay with me for many years — a Gibson Les Paul Custom 'Fretless Wonder'.

I had learned a lot from Dave Berry about stage craft and managing an audience, although my mum also taught me a lot too, back when I was just starting. I remember coming off stage once, early in my career feeling quite pleased because I'd played really well, only to walk into a serious bollocking from Mum.

"You were in your own little world staring down at your fingers looking really serious. The audience won't enjoy it unless they can see you enjoying it, I know how much you love playing, just show it!"

A great lesson well learned and from then on, I worked hard on my communication skills when performing on stage. Mum was right, it's vital to become one with the audience, it makes them enjoy it more and you come off stage afterwards feeling great.

Thanks Mum.

Dave came to see me at gig recently and I told him how much I'd learned from our time together. He seemed really surprised!

This Rock 'n' Roll Won´t Last You Know!

7
The Colonies

By 1969 we were on a roll, but big success was evading us. The then current lineup of the band was: Harvey Starr on lead vocals and valve trombone, Harvey Rose on bass and vocals, Ron Smith on trumpet, Dave Bowker on tenor sax, Alan Powell on drums and me on guitar and vocals.

We'd had a couple of singles out in the UK, 'Love Will Shake The World Awake' on MCA Records, and 'A Little Bit O' Soul' on Mercury Records, but neither made an impact on the charts.

Undaunted, we prepared ourselves for pastures new when we were offered a residency at a rock club called Jokers Wild in Freeport, Grand Bahama. A rock club in the Bahamas!

The club owners had realised there was a market aimed at American college kids who would take the short and inexpensive flight from Florida to the Bahamas to see genuine English bands and enjoy the fabulous beaches.

Dave Bowker had been offered a gig with a guy called Kirk St James, and he fancied giving it a try, so we had to quickly find a replacement. We were lucky to come across a brilliant sax player in Alby Greenhalsh, otherwise known as Alby Bear, due to his stature and big red 'grizzly' beard. Alby turned out to be perfect for us, especially with the changes ahead.

My marriage to Eileen was already in trouble, you could say she broke my heart, and this experience influenced my attitude toward women for a long time.

My focus was now truly on my career in music and although this was positive in terms of my music career it did nothing for my coming relationships.

Music would come first, and every other aspect of my life would suffer.

By now we were changing the style of music we were playing and including quite a lot of original material in the set and lots of improvisation, influenced by the new 'underground' music scene kicking off in the UK.

We changed the name of the band to Tunnel.

The flight from Manchester airport to Freeport was uneventful at first. None of us had been so far from home and the flight was longer than anything we'd experienced before. All was well until we landed in Bermuda, to refuel I guess, and a sudden bout of travel sickness hit me, resulting in a frantic grab for the sick bag — just in time... Oh well, disgraced myself but did it really matter?

We landed in Freeport at last and emerged from the plane into a blast of hot, humid air. It was wonderful.

The club owner, Dave Fishman a typical New York businessman met us, we were travelling fairly light as most of the equipment we needed was provided at the club. I just had my guitar and pedals.

An apartment was provided as part of the deal, so Dave drove us to our new home, Robin Hood Apartments in Sherwood Forest. (I'm not kidding!)

The apartment was great, enough room for us all, although I think I ended up on the couch, and a car was provided as we were far from the shops.

The next morning Dave picked us up to show us the club. Jokers Wild looked glamorous to me at the time, a typical American-style single story building surrounded by a large car park.

I made it inside first, carrying my guitar anxious to check out the equipment on stage. There was what looked to us like an amazing PA system, with large Altec speakers flown from the ceiling. Lots of gear on the stage, but I didn't like the look of the guitar amp, it was a type little known to us *Limeys* but popular in the US, a Standel.

It had a 15" speaker, totally wrong for rock music. No! we were going to be there for months, and I'd be miserable trying to get a sound out of the Standel.

Right next to the Standel on stage was a Fender Bassman, and many guitarists favoured this model for guitar. Harvey walked on stage, and I suggested he try the Standel, with its big 15" speaker. He loved it! Sorted. I would use the Bassman and Harvey would use the Standel, a great compromise.

We all spent a bit of time getting used to the gear and the room, then got the PA working for us all, and began to run through a few songs. It sounded just right, and we couldn't wait to get in front of an audience and strut our stuff.

We waited patiently for Dave to fill us in on our showtimes, and when he eventually appeared from his office at the rear of the room, he took us all a bit by surprise, telling us we started at 9:00pm and had to play 45-minute sets with short breaks, for as long as there was anyone in the club. That could mean anything really, and we soon learned that people some nights will still be there at 4:00am. We certainly needed a lot of material for this one, but it proved to be a good testing ground for our new 'underground' material.

And so it began, long nights with enthusiastic audiences, with probably too much to drink from our complimentary bar but it was great.

There was a swimming pool at the apartment, and I used to wake myself up in the morning by diving in, but Al would already be there, I think he used to sleep by the pool.

There was a long straight road to West End at the other end of the island and the Vauxhall Viva we were using used to get serious punishment from whoever was driving that day.

We soon felt comfortable on the island and began to make friends, it really was idyllic, and we were doing what we loved every night for people who were really into the music.

One problem soon arose though, when Ron announced he wanted to go home. He did leave, and that meant we didn't really have a full brass section, a problem soon solved when Alby told us he could play two saxes at once – and he could. It sounded strange but great, and it really suited our new music.

After a while I became restless during the daytime and began to explore the more remote parts of the island. I found a beach that no one else seemed to use and went there regularly on my own. I had started taking photographs with a couple of *Pentax Spotmatic* cameras that I had, and for a while that was enough to while away the days. Then I had an idea.

There was a small commercial airstrip not far from the apartment and I went there one day to check it out. There was a small cabin where the pilots would check in and I hung around for a while until a guy approached, obviously a pilot.

I asked him where he was going, and was he coming back to

Freeport today?

It turned out he was going to Nassau to make a delivery and yes, he had to be back by early evening.

Perfect! I asked if I could bum a ride and he said he would welcome the company. We walked side by side onto the area where the planes were parked and turned towards a battered looking ex-army Dakota, quite a shock as I was expecting a small civilian plane.

His job that day was to deliver a small sports car which was stowed in the plane. There was no seat for me, and I wasn't allowed in the car, so I spent the flight standing behind him hanging on for dear life inside the loudest thing I had ever heard!

The inside of the Dakota was stripped bare with nothing to deaden the sound, it was like a big, rattling tin can.

However, we did arrive safely and bade farewell until later. But I was definitely not looking forward to the return journey.

Nassau seemed a lot more 'touristy' but there was a place called the Ginza which was basically a big duty-free area.

Prices were amazingly cheap on electrical goods especially those from Japan and I bought a Sony stereo cassette recorder, and another lens for my cameras, then set off back to the commercial airfield for the return journey home.

I made a number of these flights over the next few months but none as eventful as the *Dakota* thankfully!

Something new crept into my life during this period, as I started to get more and more song ideas. I liked working alone on my songs until I felt they were good enough to play to the other guys. First, I would record them to the Sony stereo cassette recorder that I had bought at the Ginza in Nassau, then I started to get more adventurous.

I knew that in recording studios they would often create extra parts by transferring from one tape machine to another whilst adding to the original.

Why couldn't I do that? So, it was back to the Ginza via a free flight to purchase another tape recorder the same as my original one plus a few extra leads to complete the job.

There was a small sort of broom cupboard at the apartment that I commandeered as my 'studio'. I would sit in there, cross-legged with headphones on for hours recording song ideas on my crude but effective setup.

I had a suitcase for a kick drum, a tambourine covered by a teacloth for a snare drum and I would use noises from my mouth to simulate hi-hats and cymbal crashes.

I'd first record the 'drum' part, then transfer that from the first tape recorder to the second, adding a bass guitar part. Then I'd transfer the bass and 'drums' back to the first machine whilst adding a guitar part, and so on.

Working in this way I could create a complete 'band' recording of each of my songs to play to the guys so they would know what I was getting at with my ideas.

The recordings I made in this way were very crude, but effective and started a lifelong relationship with recording and studios.

The first priority when looking for somewhere to live has, from then, always been "where am I going to put my studio?"

So, life was good, and the sun was shining every day until disaster struck. I had foolishly left my treasured Gibson Les Paul Custom at the club as I felt it would be safe. I say foolishly because, yes, you've guessed it, I got a message from the club the next day to tell me it was gone.

Luckily, I did have a spare guitar to get me through the show that night, but I was absolutely heartbroken to have lost my prize possession like this. I soon got used to playing this 'new' guitar, it was a similar Gibson SG Standard so not a huge departure in terms of feel and sound although I missed my old faithful.

Then something strange, and a bit scary happened, when a guy approached me one night at the club. He had heard that my guitar had been stolen, and he said he could 'help'.

Apparently for the princely sum of $100 he was prepared to do anything — including kill someone!

He said he liked me, so he would do it for free and suggested that I make it known that I had paid him to find my guitar.

A couple of days later there was a knock on the apartment door, and when I answered it, a stranger stood there holding my Les Paul.

"Hi, I found this in the jungle, and I think its yours". Priceless!

I thanked the guy and off he went, obviously he, or the thief had heard about my deal with the gangster and decided that stealing the guitar wasn't such a great idea after all.

My Les Paul was back, and it was still in tune!

Things stayed pretty much the same at Jokers Wild until the day that Dave Fishman announced that he wanted to change the format.

He had decided that a 'Cabaret' style session might be good early in the evening to cater for older tourists.

We were shocked at first, thinking it might affect our playing times and therefore our money, but no, we were expected to provide backing for the cabaret.

Not a problem, we already had experience backing Dave Berry, Wayne Fontana, and Paul Jones so this would be the same, wouldn't it?

Absolutely not, the 'cabaret' was "Madame FooFoo", a dancer or should I say, a stripper, something entirely new for us.

Oh well, we were professionals weren't we, and nothing was impossible. In fact, it turned out to be really easy, as FooFoo was happy to do the act with us playing an extended slow blues in the background, dropping, and rising in intensity as the act progressed.

The act consisted of an extravagant entrance by this fabulous vision in full makeup followed by an erotic dance with items of clothing being removed bit by bit.

FooFoo would move among the audience, sometimes stopping to sit on the knee of a willing customer, and sometimes providing a big sloppy kiss.

Eventually back on stage FooFoo would be down to just underwear, or a bikini type outfit, reach over and rip the top off to reveal — a man!

The place would go nuts and sometimes one of the 'victims' would head for the stage for revenge, meaning FooFoo had to quickly make a beeline for the safety of the dressing room.

I don't think the FooFoo thing lasted very long, and the club management changed near the end of our time at Jokers Wild.

I recently spoke on the phone to Harvey Rose, we're still in touch after all this time thankfully, although I also keep in touch via social media with Dave Bowker and Al Powell who are both based in the U.S.

Harvey reminded me of a crazy incident that couldn't have happened any other time, I don't think.

Harvey told me of the time that the staff of the Casino in Freeport wanted us to play for them after midnight on New Year's Eve. Al said we'd do it for $100 a minute and the croupiers agreed to pay it! Crazy.

As we approached the end of our time at Jokers Wild, I guess we were all secretly wondering where we would go from here when something amazing happened.

We had just finished our last set when a guy approached us with a proposition. His name was Paul Jacobson, he was visiting the island from Florida and was in the music business in the U.S.

Paul wanted to manage us, take us to Miami, put us in an apartment and set up some shows for us via his high-profile contacts.

It didn't take long for us to say yes as you can imagine...

This Rock 'n' Roll Won't Last You Know!

8
The New World

On 5th June 1970, an expectant Tunnel entered the USA, and by the time we arrived, Paul had got us an apartment on Biscayne Boulevard and fixed up some gigs for us.

This took some quick thinking on our part as Harvey Starr had decided to leave the band and settle down with his girlfriend, who he eventually married, settling permanently in America. This left us with no lead singer, although Harvey and I felt we were up to the job.

Paul Jacobson was fine with this too. Paul had a partner, Ed Coe who ran a PA company catering for many of the major bands passing through. This was our ticket to some major opening slots for Tunnel, although there was more to it as we would find out much later.

Remember, this is the time of 'Peace and Love' in America and by 1969 there were regular 'Love-ins' across the country.

Greynolds Park was the scene in Miami on Sunday afternoon where Ed Coe would provide a large flatbed truck and full PA system for bands to use and make music for a very stoned audience.

We became a regular feature at the Greynolds Park love-ins alongside local bands and it really helped Harvey and I to get used to being 'up front' singers, I guess.

Things were moving fast, and we had an opening slot with Pacific Gas and Electric a band who were big in America at the time, featuring vocalist Charley Allen.

Then Paul hit us with the killer punch — we were opening for Jimi Hendrix at Miami Jai-Alai Fronton in front of 6,500 people, a daunting prospect for a band with two fledgling vocalists.

The date of the show was 5th July 1970, two days after my twenty-first birthday — what a present, it was really big deal for us as a band and for me as a guitar player.

Jai alai is a sport involving bouncing a ball off a walled-in space by accelerating it to high speeds with a hand-held wicker 'cesta'.

Would I be made to look stupid by one of the finest guitar players on the planet? We arrived early for the show nervous to make sure we were in plenty of time to get organised. Instructed get our gear in and ready, we set about preparing, making sure our stuff wouldn't be in the way of the main event, our hero.

A little later, Hendrix's crew arrived, and we were told to clear the building, there was an instant unpleasant atmosphere, and we were effectively thrown out until our showtime.

Not a great start to what should have been a really special — but there was more to come later when we were actually on stage later in front of a 6,500-capacity audience.

Showtime came and suddenly we were in front of our largest yet audience, nervously setting about playing material they had probably never heard before.

This was a time of experimentation in music and the audience were clearly giving us a decent chance to show what we had, and we were playing really well.

Then the power went off, and both Harvey's and my amps just shut down, silence from our side of the stage so Al just stopped drumming.

This sort of thing wasn't unusual for an opening band at that time, as sometimes if the audience were liking you 'too much' you'd be quickly shown the door.

So, Harvey and I turned to unplug our guitar leads and get off stage so the crew could get our gear off when voila! Our amps came on again!

What a surprise, this was unheard of, then Harvey's expression changed to shock, and he pointed past me to the area behind the PA stack at my side.

Hendrix's Tour Manager was kneeling behind the PA next to the main power outlet for the stage, where he had unplugged us, and Paul Jacobson was standing next to him with a gun to his head. That's why the power was back on!

So, we pulled ourselves together and played the rest of our set to a great reaction from the audience before leaving the stage for Jimi to make his entrance.

The rest of the night was a bit of an anti-climax after Paul's antics, Hendrix was unhappy on stage and didn't play like the Jimi we all knew and loved, and sadly I left the venue with mixed feelings, and I certainly didn't feel humiliated by my hero.

Despite the negatives on the night, this gig now seems like the highlight of my first foray into the music scene in America, so I'll always be grateful for the opportunity.

Since that time, I've been lucky enough to share the stage with many iconic stars of the music business in exotic locations, but this early event is very dear to me.

Onward and upward? I think our next show was with Mountain, or was it Canned Heat?
The next period is a bit of a blur so I'll tell you about it the best I can and hope not to miss anything important.

Our next important move was to spend a day at Criteria Studios, in Miami, hoping to secure a deal with Atlantic Records. It was a really big deal for us and could have changed everything, and the day seemed to go really well although the routine in the studio was a bit different to what I'd expected.

My guitar sound relied on my amp being really loud, and the guys at Criteria didn't like it. They boxed my amp in with screens around and on top of it, so I could only hear it in headphones. I hated it but had to go along with it in the end so as not to rock the boat, and the results were pretty good anyway.

We waited for feedback but were disappointed to hear bad news from a representative on behalf of *Atlantic Records* who was at *Criteria* because he'd just finished working on the Derek And The Dominos album. He had enjoyed our session but didn't feel it was right for Atlantic.

I didn't find out until later that the representative was actually Tom Dowd, a major player in the music business having worked with Ray Charles, Otis Redding, Sam and Dave, Cream, Rod Stewart, The Allman Brothers Band, and many others. Need I say more? There'll be more about him soon.

By now we were becoming aware of some worrying aspects of our setup in Miami. Being managed by Paul Jacobson, or 'Jake the Snake' as he was known, we discovered later, wasn't all it had seemed, and things began to unravel, and get worse.

Our apartment was on the 1st floor of the block and Paul had an apartment two floors directly above us. One day we were sitting around in our apartment, me on the floor and Harvey close by in front of me when I must have suddenly had a look of shock on my face.

The apartments all had balconies on one side that you could sit out on if the weather was nice, and I said to Harvey, "Paul just went past our balcony". Harvey said "oh he's probably just messing around" thinking I meant Paul had climbed from next doors balcony onto ours. "No he went that way" I said, beckoning from the ceiling to the floor.

The Police had burst into Paul's apartment, found drugs, and busted him and demanded to know the name and whereabouts of the 'main man' providing the cocaine. Paul wouldn't tell them, so they hung him over the balcony, upside down held by his ankles. They told him to tell them what they wanted, or they'd let go. Paul told them to fuck off, so they let go…

Soon we were moved out of the apartment to a new place in a rather less salubrious part of town. It was a single-story annexe to a house that I think was owned by a friend of Paul's, and not really big enough for all of us. As usual, I got the couch.

There was no air conditioning, which is not a luxury in Miami where the weather is hot and humid, instead we had a huge fan on a stand. At night each of us would, in turn, sneak over and wheel the fan to where we were sleeping where it would stay until someone else commandeered it.

We were finding out more and more about Paul's business, and it turned out that the Golden Dragon jewellery store that Paul owned wasn't really a legitimate store it was a front for drug dealing. I had a real soft spot for Paul, and I knew he liked me too, but he was dangerous.

One Keystone Cops moment I remember was when I was messing around in the house one day and Paul's car screeched to a halt on the grass outside. Paul ran inside, and out through the back door, then a black car with black windows screeched onto the grass and guys dressed in black with black shades ran to the house. They ran around the back and meanwhile Paul had circled to the front, got in his car, and screeched off, pretty soon with them speeding after.

I think this incident might have been the last straw for the rest of the guys and changes were again about to come.

Not before another, more memorable experience though, when we were invited to perform at a party for the cast after the opening of the show, *Hair*, at Coconut Grove Playhouse. A crazy, crazy day with lots of outrageous stuff going on, total madness but a welcome break from the stress we'd recently been under recently.

Meanwhile I had met Katherine, at one of the Sunday Love-ins when we were playing, and our relationship was becoming serious.

When I told her about the incident at the house, she suggested I move in with her, at her family's house. She said her parents wouldn't mind. Sure enough, they welcomed me, and I moved in there just as the guys in the band called a meeting to discuss what we were going to do moving forward.

The consensus was that most wanted to split and get away from the chaos and danger. I, on the other hand felt that we should stick it out, tell Paul to keep all the bad stuff away from us and concentrate on the music. The music came first.

I thought we had agreed to discuss this with Paul, but I was soon to discover that the others had gone. I was on my own.

At first, I didn't know what to do, but soon plucked up the courage to go and see 'Jake the Snake'. I told Paul that the guys had gone, but that I was determined to honour our arrangement. I had moved in with Katherine's family, so it was easy for me to avoid the controversial stuff and I had placed an ad in the local free ads paper for musicians to form a new band. The very first John Verity Band.

I also had other ideas on getting musicians. Paul was okay with all this, surprisingly so to be honest, and I began work on getting the new band together.

I had been frequenting the local music store Ace Music, in Miami and remembered that one of the guys working there was a bassist.

Mark Triosi was of Italian-American extraction and really did look it, I was always aware of image when it came to putting a band together and Mark looked great.

The other missing puzzle piece was a drummer, and Mark said he knew the ideal guy. Teddy Napoleon who was a real-life *Animal* from the *Muppets*, a great drummer and really extrovert to boot.

We got together and it was electric! Perfect for the sort of shows we were planning, and I couldn't have been happier.

So, we rehearsed a brand-new set, planning to debut it at the Sunday Love-in in Greynolds Park as soon as we were ready. We were expecting about 1,000 people, and it would be the first time I had fronted a band alone and the first time I'd handled all the vocals myself; I was terrified!

We were approaching the end of 1970 and so much had changed, this really was a brave new world for me and part of me was excited, but at the same time I was scared. Was I getting ahead of myself here?

The Greynolds Park gig was a great success, and we went on to open for Mountain, with a band called Blues Image also on the bill, and I was knocked out by their guitarist Mike Pinera. Blues Image had a hit single with a song called Ride Captain Ride, but Pinera left soon after to join Iron Butterfly and I don't think Blues Image survived for long without Pinera.

Despite my hopes for my new band things weren't going so well in the background. I was in the US working on a visitors' visa, flying out to Nassau to the Embassy to renew my visa from time to time. I think they got wise to me because the last time I went they only gave me a ten-day extension and warned me that if I was working, I stood the risk of being thrown out, making it more difficult to come back.

The straw that broke the camels back started with amazing news. Apparently, Tom Dowd really liked me when we did the Tunnel recordings at Criteria and wanted to make a personal introduction to Eddie Kramer with a view to us working together.

Kramer was the producer of much of Jimi Hendrix's stuff and had worked with The Beatles, Stones, Led Zeppelin and was soon to work with Kiss.

It looked like a deal was on the cards, but it suddenly went cold when 'Jake the Snake' told them he had me on a 99-year contract. He didn't, our arrangement was a handshake. The deal bit the dust.

Here's the story, in the words of my bassist at the time, Mark Troisi, who knew Tom Dowd personally:

From the memory of Mark Troisi, 1st bassist for the original John Verity Band circa Miami Fl 1970.

In 1970 through a personal relationship I had with Tommy Dowd from Atlantic records, as a favour we received and introduction and a one on one with Eddie Kramer. Tommy was an R'n'B guy so English rock was not his taste.

Eddie was in town after the death of his friend Jimi Hendrix to remix some tapes at Atlantic's studio C at Criteria studios in North Miami Beach. This was a golden opportunity at the time and one that money could not buy. Eddie was looking for new talent for the label Electric Lady.

We met Eddie downstairs at Criteria and being Eddie frickin' Kramer he was in full rock 'n' roll royalty dress complete with a paisley ascot.

He politely introduced himself and took the reel of tape John had made of three songs the band knew and played them in the small reel to reel tape room (closet). He listened intently. When finished he said, "I like it, I think the band gets in the way, but I like it, do you have a manager?" We said yes and he said he would like to meet him.

The next day we took our manager to meet Eddie and Eddie asked if he had a contract with us. The manager replied, "Yes, for the next 99 years, I own everything they do". That was that.

When I asked Tommy later what happened because we never heard back from Eddie, he told me Eddie liked the artist but not the manager.

I often wondered over the years how big a star John would have become under the guidance and support of one Eddie Kramer. I feel JV's talent as a singer/songwriter and guitarist extraordinaire, he would have become an international super star. JV always had the X factor. Timing was perfect, Eddie was the absolute man at the time and John was more than ready.

Opportunity lost.

Kind regards,
Mark

That was enough for me, and I decided to go home to England.

This Rock 'n' Roll Won´t Last You Know!

9
Time To Go Home

I didn't really make it clear to Paul as to whether my trip to England was a visit or a permanent move. I did pack all my guitars and recording gear though, leaving my amps behind sadly.

I had acquired a beautiful Sony tape machine that was capable of sound-on-sound recording to record my songwriting demos, and that just had to come with me too.

I went to the local thrift store where I found really nice, strong cases for everything including the Sony machine, and arranged airfreight for everything.

I sent my gear ahead of me so that I seemed to be travelling fairly light at the airport when I left.

January 1971 found me on the train in the freezing, miserable cold on the way to Mum and Dad's house in Wakefield.

Isn't it strange how the last part of so many train journeys seem to be through the least salubrious part of town? Oh shit, what have I done!?

I hadn't worn real shoes for a couple of years and still had my leather 'Jesus sandals' on, my feet were wet and freezing.

I have to admit that despite all this it was great to see Mum and Dad. Mum hugged my suntanned, long-haired self tight for ages whilst Dad looked on probably thinking 'silly bugger'. We unloaded my stuff out of the taxi and went in from the cold.

After a few days I was keen to get back to Bradford and start looking for musicians for a new band.

I needed somewhere to live, and after some searching found a place in Queensbury, a small town halfway between Bradford and Halifax.

Queensbury is one of the highest towns in the country and was known for getting cut off in winter, but property was cheap. I bought

16 Victoria Street on rental purchase for £450.00.

A bit like our old house in Sellars Fold, the Queensbury house was a one-up, one-down, back-to-back house, and I was assured by the seller that it wasn't due for demolition anytime soon (many small houses like this were being demolished to make way for redevelopment at this time). This was true, as the house still stands there over fifty years later.

With so many neighbours it wasn't going to be possible to record and rehearse in my new home, so a search began for a suitable place to do this, but first I needed to meet people again.

I remade contact with an old school friend, Mally Siswick, who was an accomplished bass player by now. We hadn't actually been close friends at school, I think Mally was a year above me, but I had been aware of him.

Mally told me the places to go to meet like minded people around town and this began my regular forays into Bradford hoping to find my new band.

I discovered the pubs where musicians were likely to hang out and checked the local paper for gigs to attend in the hope of finding the right people for a band.

Alongside this I was looking for a place to build a studio, and an opportunity arose to rent space underneath Queensbury Sheet Metal.

I had done a few demos on my own at home on Victoria Street and sent them off to a couple of people, but I really wanted to have a band playing on the stuff.

Steve Rowland, a record producer with a track record of getting hits with pop bands such as The Herd and Dave Dee, Dozy, Beaky, Mick and Tich had shown an interest and even offered me some session work but even he thought I'd be better with a group format. I promised to get back to him when I had further recordings.

Bare stone walls underneath a factory in one of the coldest places in the country. Great planning JV! But I bought the wood, the glue and the paint and started to make a studio for myself.

One small room for a control room and a larger space for musicians. Enough room for a drum kit, bass rig and a couple of guitarists, all reasonably soundproofed although there were no neighbours to speak of, just a cottage at the far end of the factory, and a graveyard adjacent. I never woke anyone in the graveyard!

I needed better recording equipment, and I had stuff to trade in order to upgrade. I had brought some nice guitars back with me from Miami, and although I didn't really want to part with them, needs must.

Ray Smith had a shop in nearby Shipley, where you could buy/trade all sorts of stuff. Often there were guitars and equipment there, and sometimes they had no price on, so you had to barter. I'm good at that.

Ray had a pair of Philips Pro 12 tape machines there. These machines were often used in radio stations and were built like tanks, perfect for what I needed, and I would be able to make more tracks by transferring from one machine to the other — just like Geoff Emerick did in the Beatles days at Abbey Road Studios.

I traded my Gibson Firebird 12 string guitar for the 2 Philips Pro 12s and a Vortexion mixer — I had my studio (nearly).

Norman Rose Electrical was an electrical wholesaler in Bradford, and I managed to open an account to buy all connectors and cabling I would need to finish the job.

The work was hard, and I had a near disaster working with glue in such an enclosed space but pretty soon the place was ready to go.

One day I was stopped in the street by Rowland, a guy who lived in Queensbury. He had heard that I was forming a band and he played drums. I invited him to the studio, and along with Mally we started to put some ideas down. It gave me the opportunity to try out some of the songs I had written and see if the recordings we made in the studio were up to scratch. I needed to make the studio into a viable space to record other bands in order to make a living, so it was important to get things right. The recordings sounded great!

This was a really busy period, what with trying to get a band together, and still make a reasonable living. I resorted to doing something a bit 'off the wall' but it did work out for a while.

I recorded some backing tracks at the studio and started going out by myself to do small gigs and make some money. I hooked up with an agency and although it wasn't really what I wanted to do, it served its purpose, earning a bit of cash.

A bonus that I hadn't thought of, was that other musicians were coming along to see what it was all about. That's how I met Geoff.

Geoff Lyth was (and still is) a brilliant guitarist who had a band in the Bradford area called Smokestack. Geoff and I really hit it off and soon I asked him if he would fancy joining the JV Band. This was just before I had found the space at Queensbury Sheet Metal, and I think my parting shot was that I'd come back to him when I'd found a place to rehearse.

So, I was doing the solo gigs, rehearsing with Mally Siswick and Rowland Dawson and recording a couple of local bands when I felt it was time to look Geoff up again.

Mally didn't really want to commit to being in a band full-time, so I needed to regroup as it were. I thought that Geoff's bassist in Smokestack might fit the bill, Barry seemed steady enough and got a good bass sound with Smokestack, so I went to them with a proposition.

I had approached Dave Berry to see if he was interested in me putting together a backing group for him. It would be a great way for us to make some money and tighten up the band, although musically it wasn't really where we were headed.

Dave liked the idea, so I approached Geoff and Barry, and pretty soon the JV Band Mk III was born. Early October 1972 found us rehearsing the Dave Berry set.

Dave hadn't changed the set much from when I had played with him before, so it was relatively easy for me, and the other guys learned pretty quickly.

By the end of the month, we were ready, and Dave came to the studio to check us out. We got the gig! As a bit of insurance, I decided that we should put another set together, for doing gigs on our own when Dave wasn't working and by the middle of November, we had learned a bunch of cover material and were ready to gig.

By the end of the month, we were gigging the cover band set and spending all our available time in the studio recording the original material that would eventually be our first album.

Around this time, I had also started to think seriously about how to best get the main JV band on the road once we had the material together.

I knew we needed a decent PA, and in typical JV fashion decided to build a mixer myself.

Large PA mixers were expensive, and I had discovered a company called DNA that sold impressive PA mixers, but were also prepared to sell a design, and parts to build your own.

Things like fascia plates for each channel, and the output groups would be hard to make, they needed to be sheet metal to help with rigidity and isolation, and DNA would supply those along with circuit boards. I could buy the rest of the parts, connectors, resistors, capacitors and diodes from Norman Rose, and the manager Malcolm and his assistant Dave were happy to help.

Ideally the desk needed a proper metal frame but that was out of my reach financially, so I built my own out of wood from 'The Handyman' store in Queensbury. Eventually I had my 16-channel desk finished, and it sounded really good — until you moved it!
The wooden frame wasn't really stable enough, but we stuck with it. I'm sure my old friend Geoff will have horror stories to share, but we stuck with my desk, and it got us started.

One day when I was sitting around at home putting down ideas for songs there was a knock on the door. I answered to see a young kid, asking if I was the musician who had moved into town, and I said yes of course, and he said his name was Andrew and he wanted to be in a band or be part of a road crew.

Andy Mackrill was very young, and still at school but he seemed keen to learn and I felt I could probably teach him a thing or two about the business and being on the road. I could also do with a helping hand. He only lived around the corner, so I made myself known to his parents and with their blessing took him on board.

Andy was a natural. As we began to gig regularly, he would come to my house straight from school, hop into the van, help with the gear and in the early hours we'd drop him at home. He was a real trooper, learning fast and soon became an integral part of the outfit. He stayed with me for a long time and made a great career for himself — more on that later...

Our other crew member was Malcolm Jackson, 'Mally', a diminutive likeable blues harp player turned roadie who did a lot of the driving.

Mally's size didn't stop him from carrying heavy weights but when sharing the load of a large piece of kit like a PA cabinet it did give the person on the other end a lot of trouble. I had a soft spot for Mally, and his Mum was a lovely lady, but he wasn't really cut out for this roadie thing. I think he always wished he was up front performing and in later years he did a lot of that in the Bradford area, and later around Leeds where he lived until recently when he sadly passed away.

In his later years as he became ill, he did admit to me that sometimes he would drive us, in a truckful of gear whilst tripping on LSD! No wonder he used to get lost.

Next on the shopping list was a truck. I didn't want to get a Ford

Transit van like we used to use and chose instead to get a Leyland truck. I leased it, brand new from a commercial dealership in Bradford. It was a big mistake — more on that later.

So, I thought we had everything in place but there were other changes on the horizon. We were offered a chance of a record deal with Phonogram, but as we progressed it became obvious that Rowland wasn't developing as well as we might have hoped.

The band was tightening as we gigged, but Rowland began to seem like the weak link, and I could tell that he was aware of this too. I knew that if we were going to impress record labels, we had to step up a gear and when I plucked up the courage to chat to Rowland, he admitted right away that he knew he had to go.

It was a horrible feeling; Rowland had helped us through a vital stage, but we were ready to move up and I needed the best to make that happen.

So, Rowland left the band, and at the same time Barry said he wanted to get married and didn't feel he could commit the time I needed from him to succeed. We were suddenly on the lookout for Drummer and bassist.

I already knew who I wanted to be our new drummer.
By far the best I had seen since coming back to England was Ron Kelly, he was a pocket-sized powerhouse but already in a band destined for success. I approached Ron anyway, and to my surprise he said yes, he'd love to come onboard.

I had also put the word out that we needed a bassist, and we were contacted by Gerry Smith, an experienced bass player from Leeds who had a great reputation. Gerry came over and jammed with us at the studio and it really worked, the new lineup for the JV Band was fixed.

By now Katherine had arrived from Miami and was with me at the Queensbury house. I guess it was a lot of a culture shock for her, Florida to West Yorkshire was a major change but thankfully she made friends with Margaret, who was Geoff's girlfriend, and began to settle into this new life.

My divorce from Eileen was complete and Katherine and I were married at Halifax Registry Office with little fuss and no guests to speak of. I was hoping this might give Katherine some security, but as time went on, I think she still felt out of place in this strange country. I could feel it but somehow, we didn't seem able to talk about it, and pretty soon she wanted to make a visit back home.

She did eventually make that trip back home, but on her return to me it was clear she was unhappy, and we eventually agreed to part. Katherine returned to Florida, and I never saw her again.

As usual, my head and my heart were into my music, I was frantically working on demos at home, and for the songs that seemed right for the band we were recording them at the studio.

The producer Steve Rowland really liked my home demos, there was something in there that was hitting the spot with him, and I made a few trips to his home near Marble Arch in London to discuss the possibilities of getting a record deal.

He gave me session work, which was a huge challenge but well paid, so I had to rise to it despite my lack of experience. It could be really intimidating, I remember arriving for one session at Lansdowne Studios to find that there were three other guitarists on the session, Albert Lee, Alvin Lee, and Caleb Quaye, it was terrifying!

This was a really busy period, but we still hadn't firmed up a record deal. I felt that we needed credible management, I was doing everything myself and was fairly happy with that, but I knew deep down that to get the respect we needed from prospective labels we would need representation.

I spoke to Maurice Jones, our agent at Astra in Wolverhampton to see if he could recommend anyone and he suggested I talk to Colin Blunstone. We were due to play a gig with Colin fairly soon and Maurice had already spoken about me to Colin.

After getting the okay from Colin, Maurice gave me his number, and I nervously called him for advice. Colin suggested I call Mel Collins, a successful manager in London who also looked after some credible acts at the time, including Colin, and a band called Argent!

Colin gave me Mel's number and I called his office to see if there was any interest there.

Mel asked me if there had been any interest in the band other than Astra, and I told him about Steve Rowland liking my material. That seemed to impress him, and he said he would contact Steve to see if he was serious.

Mel also asked me what gigs we'd been doing, and I was able to tell him about our support slots with ELO, and Status Quo as well as upcoming shows with Colin and the Marquee club date on our own. Things were moving fast now, and Mel agreed to manage me and come and check out the band, he had spoken to Steve Rowland, and they had a plan.

We were approaching the end of 1973 now and I really felt we were getting somewhere when a bombshell came out of the blue.

Mel wasn't interested in managing the band, in fact I wasn't to bring everyone to the office again, he just wanted to sign me as a solo artist. Steve Rowland felt the same way and they had a record company interested who had indicated it had to be just me on the contract.

I was devastated, so much work had gone into getting this far as a team, and if I dug my heels in it would all be for nothing.

At first, I just didn't know what to do, but decided to just tell the guys what was going on.

When you come to a situation like this you soon become aware of who your friends really are, they all gave their blessing to go ahead with the deal and in return I promised that as far as I was concerned it was still a JV Band project.

Any success would be shared, and I was determined that any resulting album would be called John Verity Band, not simply John Verity.

10
At Last!

On 7th November 1973 I drove to London to sign my first real recording contract. Probe Records was the UK arm of the American label ABC/Dunhill. My manager Mel Collins, producer Steve Rowland and Probe Records head Dave Chapman welcomed me to the offices of Probe, ABC/Dunhill on Piccadilly, London and the contract was signed and sealed. I felt we were getting somewhere at last!

I had already felt the benefit of being involved with Probe when I was invited to travel to London to see BB King as a fellow Probe Records artist a few weeks earlier when initial discussions were completed.

Geoff wrote in his diary at the time: *"John arrived unexpectedly and all excited at my house in the afternoon — and then we were off to see BB King in London! I know John won't have forgotten meeting him after the show, it was the happiest I'd seen him in ages! We stayed in London that night"*.

BB King was a hero to me, and it was a great honour to be on the same label, but meeting him was such a pleasure, something I'll never forget. I was in heaven.

Back in the day when you signed to major label you seemed to automatically go on their mailing list — I don't mean email!

In the ensuing months, parcels would constantly arrive, containing the latest LP releases on Probe and ABC/Dunhill, hot off the press. I was rewarded with all the latest BB King releases, and James Gang, plus the new Joe Walsh album and various others.

One of my favourites at the time was an album by Lamont Dozier, one third of the Holland/Dozier/Holland writing team responsible for so many Motown hits. *Out Here On My Own* was his own, solo album of amazing material with the best musicians and best arrangers involved, all recorded in the best studios — it's an amazing album of great material — and he's a very nice vocalist.

I was already a fan of Joe Walsh and receiving a pre-release copy of *The Smoker You Drink The Player You Get* was a welcome surprise — I still play 'Rocky Mountain Way' in my set sometimes, after all these years.

We began recording our album at Advision Studios on 17th and 18th December 1973, having stayed at the Julius Caesar Hotel the night before, the first of many stays there. We drove home to Bradford on the 18th, straight after our session, returning on the 21st and 27th to complete recording.

We weren't really so happy with the recordings as time was far too tight recording during the Miner's Strike, with the country running on a three-day week due to lack of electricity. In November 1973, the national executive committee of the Miners Union, the NUM, rejected the pay offer from the National Coal Board and held a national ballot on a strike. The vote was rejected; however, an overtime ban was implemented with the aim of halving production.

Advision did have a huge generator truck parked outside to try to keep the studio open, but we didn't have enough time to polish our performances the way we really wanted to, we were very unhappy bunnies!

The John Verity Band album was completed under the supervision of Steve Rowland, but I don't think anyone in the band was ecstatic with the result despite everyone's best efforts under the circumstances.

So that was it for now on the recording front, although the album cover was yet to be completed — the vinyl LP format gave plenty of scope to come up with something interesting.

A professional photographer had attended Advision whilst we were recording, so there were shots for the back cover, but I had to go back to the studio alone to shoot the front of the album.

It had been noticed that I sometimes got a bit overexcited at gigs, resulting in me writhing around on the floor with my trusty guitar, and they wanted to reproduce that for the cover.

I found this recreation of what was an ad-lib situation at gigs extremely embarrassing, with me plugged into an amp to try to make it look authentic whilst being photographed from every angle. The photographs were then used by an artist to draw an illustration of the act, to be used for the album cover. So, all done – or was it?

No, it wasn't, I was really unhappy with one of the tracks and really wanted to remix it, when an opportunity arose. I was staying in London on one of my trips to complete the project and decided to go for a drink in the West End. I got chatting to a guy who looked like he might be in the business, and it turned out he was.

His name was Phil McDonald and was an engineer from Apple Studios, well known for working with The Beatles, although he went on to have an amazing career with many artists.

I told Phil that I had just recorded my first album and was disappointed with the results, especially one particular track, 'Schoolgirl', which was one of most popular songs when playing live.

Phil asked me where it was recorded and when I told him Advision he offered to remix the track for me at Apple Studios if I could get the tapes from Advision. To cut a long story short, I did manage to get the multi-track tape, we remixed 'Schoolgirl' at The Beatles studio in Saville Row using the beautiful custom *Helios* console, inserted the new mix into the master, and that is the mix that is on the album.

1974 was a busy, eventful year, starting with the release of John Verity Band on Probe Records. In those days the key to a successful album launch was getting out on the road, preferably with a support slot on a major bands' nationwide tour.

Mel Collins, supported by Probe fixed up a support slot on the upcoming Argent tour, Probe having provided the required 'buy-on' payment to secure our place on the bill. Little was I to know the impact this would have on my whole career.

The tour began in January, we were treated well by the guys in Argent, although I did notice a bit of an atmosphere in their camp at times. Their bassist, Jim Rodford fixed us up with some expenses each night and I topped that up to pay for hotels and other expenses.

Jim was a lovely guy, destined to become a close friend in the near future and I was absolutely heartbroken to hear of his passing on 20th January 2018, after suffering a fall at home in St Albans. Jim's son Steve called me with the devastating news, and I was totally speechless.

Jim and I had become really close over the years working together in a number of bands through my personal ups and downs and despite all my problems Jim never judged me, such a lovely, infuriating, special human being.

I had taken out a loan to buy the brand-new Leyland truck, and leased a small car for the tour, so that me and the guys could get around quickly in the car whilst Andy and Mally drove the truck with our gear. Sometimes some of our gear went in Argent's truck and our crew travelled with Argent's crew depending on where the gigs were, with our guys helping Argent's crew in return for their help. It all seemed to be going smoothly for now.

We were doing well on the tour, with audiences giving us a decent reception most of the time which was quite unusual for an opening band — often on tours the support band would get quite a poor response from the crowd, and we managed to avoid that.

Argent were impressive, with one of the tightest rhythm sections I had ever heard, in Jim Rodford and Bob Henrit, they were stuck together like glue! Rod was and is an amazing keyboard player, with an easily recognisable style on both electronic and acoustic keyboards he remains one of my favourite players to this day.

Finally, Russ Ballard was the archetypal rock front man complete with shades, a distinctive image, and a voice to die for. Russ wrote so commercially too and was the source of much of the bands most accessible material — his hooks got you right away, classic 'ear worms'!

I remember Mel Collins coming to me after one show to point how professional, cool, and balanced their set was, and I knew it was his way of telling me to calm down a bit on stage — I did used to get a bit carried away sometimes!

As we progressed on the tour the music press reviews started to appear, and they weren't always very complimentary. I guess you needed a pretty thick skin to be in the music business at that time and I didn't, so the reviews really hurt at times as the British music press did what they loved to do — shoot you down in flames.

When I look back of course I realise how stupid I was to be so hurt, but the music press was powerful and could make or break you, so we were lucky to have some of them on our side thankfully. Some of the reviews were equally negative toward Argent, and that was some consolation in a strange way.

We really were busy during this period, doing our regular gigs in between Argent dates, trying to get to as many people as possible to promote the album to give it it's best shot.
Was it working? We were soon to find out...

We continued doing our small, local gigs alongside the work that

Maurice Jones at Astra was getting us, and venues like the Tavern in the Town in Bradford were invaluable to up and coming bands like us, as was the support of local people like Madeleine Ackroyd.

'Maddy' worked in the record department of a large retailer, Valances in Bradford town centre and she always made sure that any records by local bands were stocked in the store.

She was also very active in the live music scene and all the local bands destined for success around that time owe Maddy a lot for her invaluable help as they developed their careers.

You could always be sure that if you had an album or single out it would be stocked by Vallances – thank you Maddy, you're a star!

A big part of Argent's success was through their achievements on the 'singles' market, and despite being a full-on rock band they had also had chart success with 'Hold Your Head Up', and 'God Gave Rock 'n' Roll to You'.

Their current single 'Thunder and Lightning' was the reason they were currently on tour in the UK, with plans to go to America soon after to push it, and the *Nexus* album there.

'God Gave Rock 'n' Roll to You', and 'Thunder and Lightning' were both written by Russ Ballard, and 'Hold Your Head Up' was written by Chris White and Rod Argent.

Rod and Chris had been in The Zombies together, and when Argent was formed, Rod and Chris became the producers of the new band's recorded output.

Hit singles were still the key, despite being a rock band and I realised, too late, that there wasn't a viable hit single on the John Verity Band album. There was trouble ahead.

Still, we carried on, night after night delivering our best, and I felt the band was sounding really good. Geoff was a great guitarist but was also building his skills as a keyboard player to give us an added colour that I felt might give us an edge.

Ron and Gerry were tight, a really nice rhythm section plus we were all getting on well, and there was a good atmosphere around us, what could possibly go wrong?

Our brand-new Leyland truck was proving to be somewhat of a problem, and it started from day one… I collected it from the main dealer and drove it to my house in Queensbury, parking it outside the proud owner of my first brand new vehicle purchase.

Later in the day I was upstairs in the bedroom, looked out of the window to see that although the truck was pristine white, as ordered, the roof hadn't been painted!

The truck was tall, and you couldn't see this problem when standing next to it, you can imagine my shock, and the tone of my telephone conversation with the main dealer, although they apologised profusely, and an appointment was made to return it for a respray — including the roof!

When I first collected the vehicle, I was informed that for the first 1,000 miles it must not exceed 20 mph, due to the need for the new engine to be run-in before normal service could be enjoyed.

At the time, most commercial vehicles, and some normal cars required a running in period when the engine was new, so this was not an unusual process. This wasn't a problem for us, as we had no dates in the diary for a few weeks and I was going to gently drive around until 1,000 miles was recorded, so we could do our regular long journeys at speed.

Disaster! A couple of days later, a cancellation by another band meant we were offered a show in the northeast that I really couldn't turn down meaning we had to drive a round trip of over 250 miles at 20mph. What a great start, driving up and down the A1 with irate motorists behind us wondering what the hell we were doing in this nice, shiny new truck!

Once home, I wasted an awful lot of fuel chugging up and down to get to the required 1,000 miles under its belt by the time we were due to get out there and do a long-distance show, but I did it just in time, thinking things would be okay from now on.

This was really just the beginning of a catalogue of disasters with the Leyland, leading to fraught journeys, breakdowns, late arrivals and at least one no-show when we couldn't make it to a gig. So much for my plan to ensure reliability by buying a brand-new vehicle because buying second-hand might result in getting something unreliable… Classic!

11
The Reality Check

I guess I'm a bit of a trouper, in the old show-biz sense, because I'm pretty sure anyone seeing us perform wouldn't have known the truth, that I was worried sick about my financial situation, the lack of album sales and the obvious lack of a viable single on our album.

Our live set was strong, but with the lack of something identifiable due to our show being 100% original material was putting a major obstacle in front of us.

They used to say in the Northern clubs, "Play summat we know", and although we'd left the clubs behind, we hadn't left the attitude behind; it still exists across all of the music business regardless of genre.

These days when I play a show, I'm lucky in that I do have some stuff in my catalogue that fills that void and believe me, it's a huge advantage. I didn't have that advantage at this point unfortunately. Hold your head up, Norman!

Things can happen very quickly in the music industry, and it soon became clear that Mel Collins was losing interest although I don't really know what he had expected to happen in this very short period. There was clearly something going on at Probe too, as I was finding it more and more difficult to reach anyone on the phone and it had been so easy just a few months earlier.

The speed at which everything happened is detailed in Geoff's diary from this period, showing that from start to finish we went from the elation of getting our first album and major tour moving to the disappointment of it all crashing down in little more than six months. For me it was years of work down the pan!

From Geoff's 1974 diary entries:

25th January
First gig supporting Argent at Birmingham Town Hall. We didn't get much of a soundcheck, but we seemed to think it went well despite a cool audience response. Off to a good start...

26th January
Argent support at the Winter Gardens, Malvern. We went down better with the audience tonight and had a drink with the lads from Argent back at the hotel.

27th January
Argent support at the Guildhall, Plymouth. Had to cut our set short since everything was running late. Mally either lost or let an amp get stolen! Drove home after the gig, I'm guessing by car.

31st January
Argent support at Mountford Hall, Liverpool University.

1st February
Argent support at Edinburgh University.

2nd February
Argent support at Loughborough University. Drove home after the gig, probably by car.

7th February
Argent support at Guildhall, Portsmouth.

8th February
Argent support at Exeter University.

9th February
Argent support at Colston Hall, Bristol. Drove home after the gig for a few days, probably by car again.

11th February
JV phoned me and said there were problems with Mel Collins and thought that we would probably be leaving him at the end of the tour. I could tell that he was worried about the future at this stage.

14th February
Argent support at Apollo Theatre, Glasgow. Dave Chapman from Probe Records came up and we went back to the hotel to celebrate a good gig. Apparently, we all got pissed!

15th February
Argent support at Free Trade Hall, Manchester. The stage monitors were crackling really loud onstage, and JV couldn't hear his vocals. Bit of a struggle that night.

16th February
Argent support at Hull University. Went back home again for a few days.

21st February
Argent support at Victoria Hall, Hanley. Drove from there straight to London.

22nd February
Day off. Went shopping to Macari's Music looking for a synthesizer.

23rd February
Argent support at Pier Pavilion, Hastings. The lightshow wasn't working for us, so we played mostly in the dark! Luxury.

24th February
Argent support at Theatre Royal, Drury Lane. We'd been looking forward to this one, but everything ran late with the setup. We had no soundcheck or warm-up but played well considering the circumstances. Drove the van home that night 'cos we're off for a couple of weeks.

8th March
JV Band had a gig, but I didn't write where it was, only that I used a borrowed Marshall amp, it sounded good, and we really enjoyed the gig.

9th March
Argent support at City Hall, St Albans. A buddy of mine drove us to St Albans and back to Bradford – I can't remember why.

11th March
Argent support at Top Rank, Swansea. Drove home in van.

12th March
JV Band gig. Can't remember where because the van broke down on the way and we never arrived!

14th March
Should have been our last Argent gig tonight at Enoch's Top of The World, Stafford, but we never got there because this time the car broke down! We were all really bummed out. After recovering back in Bradford we rehearsed the show, including some of JV's new songs, 'Both Sides' and 'I'm Alive'.

14th April
Drove to London for a couple of gigs. The first one for that night never happened due to an Agency cock-up — I didn't write why.

15th April
Marquee Club London. Arrived at 2:00pm as arranged, but we couldn't get set up until 6:45pm and doors opened at 7:00pm. Obviously, we didn't get a soundcheck and we were all mighty miffed. The gig didn't go very well, although we played reasonably well, considering. Drove home that night.

16th April
JV phoned me in the evening saying that 'they' don't want Ron and Jerry. Can't be sure, but I think 'they' were Probe, rather than management, but that might be wrong. Anyhow, you were obviously upset and said you didn't know what to do after all we had been through together and asked me not to say anything to them about it for now.

18th April
Had a meeting at your house where JV told Ron and Jerry the news. Stunned silence all round. Still had a few gigs left yet, so we had to carry on…

21st April
Played at ICI, Runcorn. I wrote that we played 'better than ever'. Rehearsed the new songs and 'Don't Knock It' for the next three days. I don't know what happened, but I wrote in my diary that I was 'worried about Jerry' and seem to recall him being really bummed out or pissed. Maybe both.

3rd / 4th May
More rehearsals.

26th May
Had a gig but can't remember where.

7th June
JV came to my house to let me know we were probably going to have to wind up the band. There must have been something wrong with the truck because he said we couldn't afford the deposit for a new one, and there didn't seem to be a way out. So, the gig for the 9th had to be cancelled. JV mentioned he'd had an offer to join Argent, so was going to London that week to see how things went at a rehearsal.

21st June
Played at the Cavern, Liverpool.

23rd June
Played somewhere in Accrington.

29th June
Played again, but I wrote even less about it this time, so I'm not sure where, but think it was at the Tavern in Bradford. Only wrote that we were all really upset because we went down really well, but the party was over.

4th July
Last gig at Bierley Labour club, Bradford.

Despite all this, there were positive things happening for me, but aside from the band unfortunately, with more sessions coming in from Steve Rowland when he booked me to play on some 'Family Dogg' sessions.

Family Dogg was a project that Steve had put together, and it consisted of mostly seasoned session musicians and other guests (like me), with Steve often doing lead vocals on many of the tracks.

We always recorded in great studios, and I learned a lot, both technically and as a guitar player. Steve was generous to be honest, as I probably wasn't up to the standard of a lot of session players for this sort of material although I did raise my game enough to be invited back for more.

Colin Blunstone called my one day to ask me if I'd be interested in doing a session with him, I guess he must have been impressed when we opened for him and of course I said I'd love to do the session.

The day came and I took my guitar and my little Fender Champ amp down to Central Sound Studio in Denmark Street, in London's West End to play on a projected Colin Blunstone single 'Last Bus Home' and another track for the B-side.

The producer on the session was Hugh Murphy, a lovely guy and we hit it off right away,
Hugh created a great atmosphere, and the A-side session went so well that he seemed to let me do whatever I wanted on the B-side.

The track ended with quite a long, improvised guitar solo, and Hugh just let me play to my hearts content until the track ended, I loved it!

I don't think Colin's version of the single was ever released, I think due to contractual issues, but I was listening to the radio one day and was surprised to hear a new version, this time by Suzi Quatro renamed 'Rolling Stone' with a whole new set of lyrics.

I was disappointed of course that my improvised solo didn't make it on to vinyl but pleased to get a phone call soon after from Hugh, inviting me to come and play on a new album he was producing by Tim Rose, the American artist whose biggest success was with the song 'Morning Dew'. Rose also claimed to be responsible for the original version of 'Hey Joe' a huge hit for Jimi Hendrix. The sessions were at IBC Studios in Portland Street, London, my first visit there and the other guitarist on the sessions was Andy Summers, soon to reach stardom with The Police.

JV Band wise I discovered why the Probe Records situation had gone sour so quickly. Probe was no more because ABC/Dunhill had ceased their relationship and removed their catalogue of albums and singles, forming instead a new UK label Anchor, with Ian Ralfini, already a major player in the music business.

I was invited to discuss my future with Anchor, but they weren't interested in taking the current JV Band album or picking up on my newest material. That, and the mounting debt pretty much sealed the demise of my band with Geoff, Ron and Jerry in one fell swoop.

Anchor had immediate success with a track called 'How Long' by Ace, written by, and featuring Paul Carrack who of course had a glittering future ahead, although there wasn't a great deal more from them until the labels demise in 1978 following the acquisition of ABC/Dunhill by MCA Records.

It wasn't too long before I was beginning to pick myself up a bit and had begun discussions with some guys from a band called Coast (or was it Freeway?)

I felt that the only way to keep a JV Band going was to pick up an existing lineup to join me, avoiding the responsibility of doing, and providing everything myself.

They were already a three-piece band, Coast; Peter (Biff) Byford on bass, Paul Quinn on guitar and I believe the drummer was John Walker.

It's all a bit vague and I believe we may have done one gig together and were then sitting in my house in Queensbury discussing our next move when the second call came from Argent's management offering me the chance to join the band.

I accepted with the 'New JV Band's' blessing, so this lineup never grew its wings although a couple of years later they did approach me to help them get a record deal and produce their first album as Saxon. More on that later...

This Rock 'n' Roll Won´t Last You Know!

12
New Horizons

The rest of the year was spent making regular trips to St Albans to rehearse, and to London's CBS Studios to add my bits to the new Argent album *Circus*, although my contributions were all vocal, as I didn't play guitar on *Circus* which felt really odd — there may be trouble ahead!

It became clear that I couldn't remain living in Queensbury, so management suggested I share a house with Argent's tour manager/sound engineer Don Broughton in London.

It seemed like a good idea, so I agreed although there were a couple of things to sort out first before committing to that, as I had a serious relationship with my girlfriend Pam to consider and Andy Mackrill was still officially working with me.

Mally had gone back to his first love as a guitarist/blues harp player and was happy enough with the change, but Andy really seemed to want to stay with me.

I approached management to explain that I had my own guitar tech, and wanted to bring him with me but was told there were no vacancies on the crew, so I offered to pay Andy's wage for a trial period if they would cover his expenses and they agreed.

Although Pam and I weren't living together at Queensbury — she was still living with her parents in Bradford, she agreed to move to London with me, together with Andy.

We found a three-bedroom house in Colindale, North London, where Myself, Pam, Andy, Don and his wife could live and made a fresh start.

There was some beautiful stuff on *Circus*, although the band had made a change in direction away from the really commercial stuff that Russ Ballard had contributed, and I did wonder at the outset if that was a mistake.

It quickly became very clear that this was an entirely different league that I'd moved into with such amazing, complete players and once again I knew I had to raise my game.

I had noticed the quality of the original lineup when we opened for them of course. but standing there playing in the same band was a totally different kettle of fish — and very scary.
The arrangements were much more complex than anything I'd encountered before, with time and tempo changes coming out of nowhere — there was one section of 'Music from the Spheres' that I rarely got right in concert.

We rehearsed at the Pioneer Youth Club in St Albans regularly to get the next tour show in shape and then went to Ealing Town Hall for two weeks to do final dress-rehearsals with full PA and lighting.

Andy was doing really well on the crew, and was offered a permanent job, although I soon realised that he really wanted to be a drum tech.

Bob was impressed with Andy so I agreed to a change — Andy would work for Bob and one of the crew, Pete, would be my guitar tech. Sorted!

My first show with Argent was at Bournemouth Winter Gardens, opening a UK tour that was to last until 21st December with a triumphant homecoming gig for the band at St Albans Civic Hall. I was the only 'foreigner' in the band!

Bob always used to say they'd saved me from going down t'pit when they offered me the Argent gig!

We did further sporadic UK shows until February, when we hit the road in America for the new Argent lineups first US tour, on February 21st at The Capitol Theatre, Passaic, New Jersey. There were three bands on this show, American band Kansas opened, we went on second and Queen headlined, although Brian May (now Sir Brian May) came into our dressing room afterwards exclaiming 'Why aren't you headlining?'

Queen were amazing that night, never afraid to try new things in live performance, so, so tight, great vocals and harmonies and for me the killer blow was that amazing guitar sound. Wow!

This short tour ended in Canada at the Massey Hall, Toronto on 24th March and we returned home to prepare for the official launch of the new album *Circus*.

By now the band was being managed by Good Earth Management's

Roger Myers, and he had rather grand ideas of us doing a special circus themed show at London's Roundhouse to launch the album.

The tracks on *Circus* were all related to various circus acts and as we rehearsed various acts devised their routines around us as we played. It was bizarre but it worked!

The 13th April show at the Roundhouse sold out and went incredibly well on the night with everyone in the band at the top of their game, I was proud to be involved — despite some of the unexpected pyrotechnics scaring the shit out of me!

Jim said at the time that with such a special show, we must have cracked it, launching the new album and new lineup properly at last, and this seemed to be confirmed when whilst driving home, he heard a DJ from a London radio station who had been there raving about it.

How wrong can you be... despite the sold out show we were careful to make sure that the music press were properly represented, sending out free passes to all the papers we thought would be interested. After the initial euphoria you can image how we felt to see stinking reviews across all the extremely powerful music press the following week.

They could make or break you in those days, and they were clearly trying to break us, the miserable bastards.

I think the common feeling amongst everyone in the band at the time, despite us soldiering on with yet another album and tours, was that this could sadly be the beginning of the end.

We were due to start our next UK tour in June, but Bob called me one day to say he was seriously ill, he had contracted hepatitis and would be unable to work meaning the tour was off.

We were also due to start recording a new album, to be called *Counterpoints* and it looked like we might have to cancel that too, until I got a call from Jim to tell me that he'd just had a call from Phil Collins, the drummer from Genesis, who had heard that Bob was unwell.

Phil was a big fan of Bob's playing and offered to step in and cover for Bob until he was well enough to come back, an amazing gesture that we were going to put to Bob to see how he felt about it.

Bob was absolutely fine about it, and Phil played drums on five tracks on *Counterpoints*, until Bob was well enough to join us in the studio for the remainder — there's even one track where Phil plays the first part and Bob takes over later, classic!

We recorded the basic tracks at John Kongos Studio, with our usual producer Chris White at the helm assisted by Tony Visconti, and I did some of my vocals there before we moved to Tony's studio in West London to complete the vocals, add my guitar parts and complete the mixing.

We began the UK Counterpoints tour on September 7th, 1975, at Guildford Civic Hall and ended the tour at Reading University on 29th October before heading to America for what was sadly to be Argent's final US tour.

Our new US Agents Capricorn persuaded us that the way bands were touring now was in a vehicle with bunks so that long drives could be accommodated without stopping for hotel stays, and we fell for it!

We picked up the vehicle in New York I believe, a large Winnebago which was already a little the worse for wear to be honest, and headed for Montreal, Canada for our show, returning to New York for the next one.

On our drive through the extreme New York State winter weather, we were taking turns to drive, and Jim was driving when disaster almost finished us for good. It was snowing heavily, and large trucks were approaching us heading in the opposite direction.

As they passed alongside us as we were running through a steel bridge, the air displacement pushed us away from the centre of the carriageway, making us hit the supporting bridge posts with the side of our vehicle, ripping off the awning that was fitted to the side of the Winnebago.

This was just the beginning of the tour, and we had many thousands of miles to go on the winter roads, looking back I think that it was only the fantastic reaction we'd had in Montreal the night before that kept us going. Musicians are nuts.

In New York we were playing the Beacon Theatre, a venue where Argent had always been popular, so flushed with the success in Canada we took to the stage feeling confident only to find that there were serious problems with Rod's rig, it sounded terrible and obviously as keyboards where such an intrinsic part of our sound it really screwed up the show.

We battled on, but the crowd response was less than enthusiastic, and we hit the road after the show feeling tired and down.

The next couple of gigs on the East Coast were well received and we played well, with a 2,600-mile journey by road from Clarksburg Virginia to Seattle Washington for the next show to look forward to…

We had five days to make this journey, virtually coast to coast and the Winnebago had begun to become unreliable, hard to start at times, and eventually breaking down for no apparent reason.

Our driver obviously couldn't make the whole drive, so we started taking it in turns to take over from him as we drove through snow blizzards in Pennsylvania and the extreme heat of Death Valley — I remember us pulling into a truck stop one night and offering to take over the driving for the next leg of the journey.

I went inside, bought a box of *No-Doze* tablets, the type that truckers used to take to keep themselves awake on long journeys and took the lot, in an attempt to make up for lost time.

We all piled back into the bus, and I took the wheel, wide eyed from the *No-Doze* overdose, turning the ignition to... nothing!

The bonnet (hood) was opened to find out what the problem was, and our tour manager returned to us to say, "better get some kip lads, the alternator has packed in, and we can't get help until the morning".

I lay in my bunk, wide eyed and legless, grinding my teeth until next morning when the mechanic arrived, by which time I was in no fit state to drive, I think Jim took over again and we were off, on our way for our show at the Paramount Theatre, Seattle for the first of a string of dates as special guests to Steppenwolf.

These dates went really well, and as we travelled through Oregon and California, we were treated properly so no onstage problems and the guys in Steppenwolf were friendly, especially the Guitarist Bobby Cochran, a nephew of the rock 'n' roll legend, Eddie Cochran.

Next was a three-night residency at the Starwood Club, LA where we headlined. I remember coming off stage one night wondering why Bob had looked a bit uncomfortable during our set. I asked him what was wrong, and he said, "did you notice the guy taking pictures at the front all night — especially of me and the drums?" I said I'd seen him, why? Bob said, "it was Billy Cobham!" no pressure then, Bob!

Next, we headed east, across the south to do our own shows in Texas and the final ever gig of this new Argent lineup in Dothan, Alabama on the bill with Steppenwolf once again, and Savoy Brown.

Our final drive was south through Florida to Miami and our flight home, with the suspension of the Winnebago now collapsed, making it lean crazily to one side, and a doom-laden atmosphere inside as we were all feeling privately, I think, that this might be the end of the new Argent lineup.

John Grimaldi's behaviour had become pretty poor, and one night he even threw his double neck Gibson up in the air, letting it crash to the ground in front of a large audience to our horror, leaving me to run offstage to get my guitar so we could carry on without him. A pretty extreme way to hand in your notice you might say, although he seemed to be forgiven — I wasn't party to those conversations, but he carried on for the next shows.

I had already decided some time earlier that I would form my own band to run alongside Argent, I think the seeds of this idea were planted when Phil Collins was working with us in the studio when he mentioned Brand X, his band that ran alongside his work with Genesis.

I had mentioned this to Bob and Jim as we travelled across America and we had agreed that it was a great idea, and one that we should do together. I had already written material that wouldn't have worked for Argent but would be good for a more rock-based power trio.

On 18th December 1975, we decided to end Argent.

I didn't have any firm future plans as yet, although Bob, Jim and I were determined to put a project together, however word had obviously got out that Argent had ceased to exist and by the time I'd got back to England the offers started to come in.

The first approach was from Aerosmith's management asking me if I'd be interested in joining a band being formed by Brad Whitford, one of the band's guitarists.

Aerosmith had either split or were taking a break and the individual members were obviously putting together projects of their own, however once discussions began it didn't feel that it was right for me, so I politely declined the offer.

Christmas was coming, and I was home again doing what all families do over the Christmas period, when on New Year's Eve the phone rang, I answered, surprised to hear from Andy Fraser, former bassist with Free.

Andy said he was putting a band together and wanted me to be involved, could I come over to his place to rehearse — tonight!

I explained that it was New Year's Eve, and I was with my family, but he was really insistent, saying he had a keyboard player and drummer on the way, and he really wanted to get started.

I must admit that I was really intrigued and said I'd call him back soon after I had spoken to my wife, Pam who was sitting next to me already working out what I was going to say. Pam reluctantly agreed that it might be a good career move so I called Andy back, got his address and suddenly realised that all my equipment was still being shipped back from the U.S.A, so a quick call back to Andy to see if there was an amp for me and I set off with one of my spare guitars...

I arrived at Andy's place a couple of hours later, he answered the door and led me to a nice rehearsal room, but I was surprised to find that there was no-one else there. Andy said they were on their way, and could I just sing for him... strange.

So, I sang and played alone with him sitting there until he excused himself saying he'd be back in a minute. The minute turned to ten, then fifteen and I started to get impatient so went to find him, wherever he was.

I opened a door which led to a kitchen, where Andy was sitting on top of a refrigerator, smoking a joint at which point I turned and went back to the rehearsal room, retrieved my guitar, and went home. What was all that about?

This Rock 'n' Roll Won't Last You Know!

13
Ch-Ch- Changes

With 1976 came our new project, Pam and I had bought a house in Northwest London a while earlier, a small two-bedroom place but it was detached, so ideal for rehearsing a band in private, and of course I had recording equipment...

We started recording demos of new material, the first one being one of my songs, 'Easy', and then a bunch of stuff with all of us contributing — very democratic!

We had been really impressed with the organisation behind Queen when we toured America, and as luck would have it, Bob already knew one of the Directors at their management company, Trident.

Once I had finished polishing and mixing the demo tracks, we took them in to Trident's offices in London's West End for a meeting. They liked what they heard, a deal was struck, a contract signed, and we were off and running again, thankfully... as we all had families, and mortgages to pay.

In May we began recording at Trident Studios, St Annes Court in the West End of London just around the corner from the Marquee Club, and the fabled Ship pub where the bands of the day tended to congregate.

Trident was one of the first independent studios in the country, as up until now all the major recording studios were linked to or owned by the major labels.

Norman and Barry Sheffield acquired a suitable building in London's West End. St Annes Court ran between Wardour Street and Dean Street so was ideally situated near the heart of the major UK music industry players.

The studio complex was on four floors, with the main 'tracking' studio on the ground floor, the control room looking over a large 'live' area with enough room for a small orchestra, or more often, a full band laying tracks down for sweetening later.

Trident's most famous clients by far were The Beatles, who, tired of working at Abbey Road, decamped to Trident on a number of occasions — on one occasion recording 'Hey Jude'.

Up on the first floor was the 'remix' room, with a fully equipped control room and a small overdub/vocal booth for building up the remaining tracks to add to the recordings made downstairs.

On the second floor was the 'cutting room', where clients could take their master tapes to be transferred to the lacquer that would be used to manufacture vinyl albums and singles — the age of CD had not arrived yet!

The Trident offices were next, with finally, on the 5th floor, the maintenance department, meaning there was everything you might need to create manufacture and market a product under one roof.

Norman Sheffield was the partner overseeing our project, and he appointed Dave Thomas to look after our day-to-day business. We were happy to have a 'home' again and it all seemed very professional, with the bonus of our management owning Trident Studios and a film company, Trillion.

We were debating whether to call our new band a name, or to use our own names as we all had a bit of profile.

Eventually we decided to do both, the intention was to call the album *Phoenix* — because we were rising from the ashes of Argent, get it? and the band would be called Henrit, Rodford and Verity, although when the album came out everyone picked up on "Phoenix" and that became the actual name of the band.

We signed a production deal with CBS Records — we didn't need to sign directly to a label because Trident were providing the studio time and billing it to us, to be paid out of royalties, the main advantage being that we had creative control of the material to be used on the album. Basically, we provided the finished product and CBS released it on their label.

During a break in recording Bob, Jim and I were booked to go to Château d'Herouville in France to record an album with Dave Courtney, who had written songs for Leo Sayer and Roger Daltrey. Dave wanted to record his own album away from the UK for tax reasons.

The studio later became known as the 'Honky Château' when

Elton John recorded his album of the same name there.

We were booked for nine days to record the album from start to finish, and the studio was residential, having lots of accommodation, plus a swimming pool and tennis courts.

There were mic-lines down to the swimming pool and I even recorded some of my guitar parts sitting down there!

The château grounds were covered in gravel around the building itself and one evening I could hear footsteps outside. Bob called to me from his room "look outside", and when I did, I could see David Bowie and Iggy Pop standing in the moonlight, casually smoking cigarettes.

I chatted to David at breakfast the next day and he was really friendly, relaxed and seemed at home at the château, I wondered if he was there checking out the studio, or just having a break as he was currently on tour in Europe.

With our stint at the château finished, we returned home to make a promotional video at Pinewood Studios, and then prepared for rehearsals at a farm in Hertfordshire, intending to do some warm-up dates in the UK before touring with Aerosmith across the UK and Europe.

We played well on the Aerosmith tour, but the music scene was changing rapidly, as Punk Rock began to take over, and I realised that our timing was terrible, forming an old-school, straight-ahead power trio with the visual image that we had. I had even noticed that some musicians of our era were starting to adjust the way they looked to conform to the 'new look'. I thought it was pathetic.

The *Phoenix* album wasn't selling as well as we had hoped, and CBS were getting worried. In the meantime I had some session work to distract me when Colin Blunstone called to ask me to contribute to his *Planes* album by adding vocal harmonies.

Colin is one of my all-time favourite vocalists and a lovely guy to boot, so I of course agreed, and the fact that Rod Argent and Russ Ballard were also on the sessions was a bonus.

The tracks were recorded at Trident Studios, handy for me, and were produced by Gus Dudgeon, well known for producing Elton John and David Bowie.

I wasn't to know at the time that Phoenix would soon sign to Rocket Records, and that Gus Dudgeon would produce some of my recordings many years later.

A few weeks later, meeting to work out a way forward for Phoenix we all agreed that we'd go back into the studio and make a start on a new album, it was January 1977 and Punk was strong, meaning we had to come up with something special.

In the meantime I had become friendly with Ray Minhinnett, a brilliant guitarist who I'd first met when we were neighbours in Colindale, and I had the feeling that it might be time to change the Phoenix lineup a little, maybe it might work with two guitarists, as I would normally add extra guitar parts on our recordings that were then missing when we played live.

I discussed the idea with Bob and Jim, and they agreed, feeling that this small change would give us more scope, especially as the new recordings we had completed all had more than one guitar part already.

We played one more show as a three-piece, a UK TV show called *Supersonic*, still promoting the first Phoenix album — we played my song, 'Easy' which CBS had released as a single, before getting Ray onboard in January 1977 to continue the recording of the second album.

We had already completed six songs with the three-piece lineup, so Ray and I began writing together at my place to get some material ready for the remaining tracks.

I was very aware that we still needed a strong single for the album, so I was also on the lookout for possible covers too.

By the end of the year, we were ready, with new material written, and I also thought that we should try a brand-new version of Rod's beautiful song 'Time of the Season'. Speaking of beautiful songs, Chris White contacted me around this time, with one of my favourite songs of all time 'When My Boat Comes In', so beautiful that it's hard to sing without getting too emotional and bursting into tears! I'm a big softy you know.

There was a short, forced break due to Trident being booked up already by another band, but no break for me as it happens.

Around this time I had an endorsement deal with *Fender*, for guitars and amplifiers and they approached Bob, Jim and I to do a tour of the UK demonstrating their products at a series of 'clinics' where I would demonstrate *Fender* guitars and amps, Jim *Fender* basses and Bob *Rogers* drums which were manufactured for Fender.

We fitted the tour around the sessions at Trident, putting together the new material that we hoped would rejuvenate the Phoenix project.

In the middle of this tour something happened that would again force us to change, when Jim asked us to get together because something had come up — he had been offered a tour playing bass for The Kinks which might become a permanent offer, what did we think?

Of course there was no way we would stand in Jim's way, so early in March 1978 Phoenix were bass-less — if The Kinks gig turned out to be permanent for Jim.

We carried on recording without him but in early August whilst they were doing dates in Belgium, The Kinks offered Jim the gig permanently. We, of course gave our blessing and Jim became a Kink.

Another blow was coming — whilst we were recording this new material, Dave Thomas came to us with bad news, CBS had decided not to continue with the Phoenix project, frightened that Punk had wiped out the more conventional rock market. We were label-less again.

So, we shelved the album that I have always fondly remembered as Phoenix II and started work on a new version of the band, keeping 'Time of the Season' as it was the first one with the new lineup.

We soon had some good news thankfully, when Rocket Records, Elton John's label expressed an interest but wanted to start with a single, having heard a work-in-progress copy of our version of 'Time of the Season', so we got straight back into the studio to finish it off.

The Head of A&R at Rocket Lem Lubin was an old friend of Bob's, they had been together many years earlier in the band Unit 4+2, for their 'Concrete and Clay' hit single which Russ Ballard also played on.

Lem joined us in the studio as we worked on 'Time of the Season', trying to make it as commercial as possible.

Jim had already created an amazing bass line on fretless bass before he went off with The Kinks, and Ray and I began adding contrasting guitar parts.

It really seemed to work, Rocket Records agreed, and it was released as a single with my song 'Daylight Robbery' on the B-side.

Colin Blunstone also called me around this time to book me to do backing vocals again, this time on his *Never Even Thought* album, this time produced by Bill Schnee, an American producer responsible for much of Neil Diamond's catalogue. We worked on the tracks at Trident Studios again, for Rocket Records.

With a break from Phoenix recording to give Rocket time for marketing I had a surprise call that would give me another nice project to work on, when Russ Ballard got in touch to ask me to do some studio work with him, and of course I accepted.

Russ was working on songs at Livingston Studios in New Barnet when the engineer unexpectedly went into hospital, leaving Russ without help.

The studio was well designed, with equipment I was familiar with, and Russ knew that I was a capable engineer and producer, able to help him finish his current project, leading to the call.

I fell in love with Livingston as soon as I started playing some tapes to familiarise myself with the setup, it just sounded right, and the lovely old Neve mixing console was pure Rolls Royce. Everything about Livingston was dead right for recording my kind of music, with the Neve, great monitoring, a good selection of the best microphones and a great sounding 'live room'. I was loving it!

Russ was much more disciplined with regard to working days than anyone I'd worked with before, he liked early starts, and would usually finish late afternoon, leaving me to mix whatever track or tracks we had completed that day, later in the evening. We were a real conveyer belt at this time!

Soon after I first started doing sessions at Livingston I enquired if there was a decent Indian restaurant in town, to be advised to use the Chinese instead, although there was an "Indian around the corner you can try".

I'm not a huge fan of Chinese food so decided to give the Indian a try, and following the directions found the 'Golden Tandoori'.

As I walked through the door I was greeted warmly, led to a table and before I could say anything was greeted by the pop of a cork and the waiter exclaiming "bottle of *Blue Nun* Sir?"

Clearly, I had been mistaken for another customer, however the food was great and over the next couple of years I was a regular customer — always greeted by the words "bottle of *Blue Nun* Sir?" I hated *Blue Nun* but didn't have the heart to tell them.

Livingston was a 16-track studio, well known for a lot of folk music albums, and the regular engineer, Nick Kinsey was a brilliant engineer although of course currently hospitalised.

I didn't know how long he was going to be unavailable, or how long I was going to be available, so it was convenient that Russ had such a good, organised routine allowing us to get a lot done in a short time.

Russ would come into the studio each morning with two or three song ideas, and by the end of the day they were complete, and mixed ready to go out for prospective clients to cover.

Sometimes Russ would have a brief, it might be to write a song for a particular artist or band, so we would try to aim a song to fit their style, and I would similarly aim to get the right sound to suit them, it was challenging but really interesting.

I was approached by Russ's manager, John Stanley one day with what I thought was a challenge. John said that it seemed a shame that we were treating the recordings as demos, and why couldn't Livingston upgrade the equipment so that we were able to make finished master recordings?

I think that clients had often said to him that they would really like access to the multi-tracks that we had recorded so that they could simply add their artist and save a lot of time and expense. I said I'd see what I could do.

Livingston was equipped with a 16-track 'Studer' tape machine utilising 2-inch tape, although things had moved on and people expected 24-tracks on 2-inch tape as a recognised standard.

My home studio was also 16-tracks on 2-inch tape, although I was loving working at Livingston so much that I was prepared to sacrifice my own setup for the greater good, as it were.

Nick Kinsey was now out of hospital, and we had become friendly so I approached him with an idea — we could combine my own setup with the Livingstone 16-track gear and trade up to 24 track, with me acquiring shares in Livingston Studios for my contribution.

Nick and the other shareholders agreed, I negotiated a deal and became a shareholder, and we traded up to an Ampex 24-track tape machine and some other upgrades to make us competitive on the current studio scene.

A bonus was that the Ampex machine we had found also had a 16-track headblock meaning if our current and older clients wanted to work on their 16-track tapes we could still cater for that. It was simply a case of unplugging the 24-track plug-in headblocks and replacing them with the 16-track alternative. Perfect!

Due to family matters, there was a break planned in for Russ's sessions at Livingston, so I was surprised to hear from John Stanley asking if I was available for a new project.

I said yes, to be told that Russ was producing some sessions with

Ringo Starr at Sweet Silence Studio in Copenhagen, and would I play guitar on them?

The sessions would be 'open ended' meaning that there was no fixed end date, but I knew I could move other stuff around to make it work, especially for such an important project — the chance to work with Ringo!

I packed my trusty red *Samsonite* case for an extended stay and waited for the car with Bob Henrit already on board to collect me, and drive to Heathrow airport for the flight.

We stopped off to pick up Chas Hodges, who was booked to play keyboards on the sessions, and he got on board carrying a Tesco shopping bag with a change of socks and underpants, and some cans of beer, safely stored!

Bassist Dave Wintour was also on the sessions but had made his way directly to the airport, where we all met and as usual headed for the bar until check-in time.

As we queued for check-in the extremely 'camp' guy at the desk seemed nervous as we worked our way toward the front, and Bob seemed a little amused but didn't say anything until we were on the plane, after the swiftest check-in I had ever experienced.

Once on the plane, Bob explained that the guy who had checked us in was an old schoolfriend, who he hadn't met for many years.

There had been no sign at school that he might be gay, and clearly, he hadn't enjoyed bumping into Bob like this today, not that it was a problem to us.

Anyway, here we were, safely on the plane, heading for a real landmark in all of our career's, making a record with Ringo Starr of The Beatles. Wow!

On arrival in Copenhagen we were surprised to find that there was no-one to meet us, so we called the studio for an update, to be told that we were a day early, but that we'd be picked up as soon as possible, and our hotel reservations would be updated, allowing for the extra nights stay.

Again, we decamped to the airport bar to wait, and I decided to play it safe and sample draft beer thinking it was probably the weakest option.

Carlsberg Elephant looked a good choice, confirmed when I tasted my first glass to find it wasn't particularly strong tasting at all. How wrong can you be!

The conversation soon became a little louder as we began to swap stories and generally joke about in true Rock 'n' Roll fashion, and by the time our car arrived we were probably ready for bed!

We were delivered to the hotel, to be told that Ringo was going to take us out for a meal that night, so that we could get to know each other and have a relaxing evening before getting down to work tomorrow, it was time to sober up double quick.

A nice shower and change of clothes seemed to do the trick, and we all met in the hotel lobby ready for a bite to eat.

Ringo said the evening was on him, and he had chosen a nice restaurant to start with, meaning he must have something planned for after our meal.

The fact that the meal was 'on him' was a great relief, as the prices on the menu at the plush restaurant that Ringo had chosen, were extortionate!

It was really nice to start the project like this, Ringo was charming and friendly, and we all felt at ease now, looking forward to making a start in the morning — the evening wasn't yet finished.

After the meal we were led to a club, already busy but with an area held back for us, with table service from the bar.

I was quite full from eating our meal, so decided against drinking more beer, ordering a *Jack Daniels* instead.

The waiter returned with our order a few minutes later, and put a full bottle of *Jack,* with a glass and tumbler of ice in front of me. Oh no...

The evening was jolly as you can imagine, and I don't remember getting back to the hotel, but I awoke safely in my bed next morning feeling diabolical.

Now really worried about the day ahead I decided to get to the studio first so that I could prepare myself properly before everyone else arrived.

I showered quickly, dressed, and made my way to the studio, guitar in hand, knowing that an amplifier specified by me would be waiting for me when I got there.

The studio was open, but very quiet when I got there, just a maintenance guy in the control room setting everything up for our session, so I chose my place, set up my gear, tuned my guitar and went looking for somewhere to hang out until the rest of the guys arrived.

There was a 'Green Room' area, and still feeling terrible I thought I might find somewhere to lay down for a bit until everyone else arrived.

I did find a quiet place, certain I wouldn't be disturbed and curled up for a few minutes rest.

I awoke startled, and panicked, not knowing what time it was, pushed the door of my refuge open to see that it was dark outside, shit, I'd blown it!

I heard voices approaching, one of them Ringo's and waited for the bad news, but as they came around the corner Ringo spotted me and said, "Oh you're early John I don't think we're ready for you yet".

Nobody had given me a schedule, and it seems I wasn't needed for the first session as it was done with the Copenhagen Philharmonic, and they didn't need me until later.

Relieved, I was going to be a good boy for the rest of the trip, not wanting to blow this amazing opportunity, and as we began to play through the songs in the studio it was good to feel my guitar in my hands and get on with some playing.

To start with, we were to record four songs that Russ had written, 'On The Rebound', 'She's So In Love', 'As Far As We Can Go' and 'One Way Love Affair', and I think we got the first two down before the end of the day, with basics for the second two completed the following day. During a break on the second day, everyone except me left the studio for a while, and I was sitting, just 'noodling' on my guitar alone when Ringo and Chas wandered in.

We sat chatting for a while, and then Ringo sat at Bob's kit and began to play a little, until Chas joined him, playing the studio piano, so I quickly picked up my guitar again and began to join in.

Suddenly we were playing for real, 'Blueberry Hill', 'Whole Lotta Shakin'', and lots of other Rock 'n' Roll standards as I frantically tried to attract the engineer's attention through the control room window, hoping we could record this.

The guy just looked blankly at me, and sadly nothing was recorded, but for me it was an amazing experience, one I'll never forget.

Once everyone returned to the studio after the break, we continued with the job in hand, although clearly something was not right with Russ, he was really quite detached and communication wasn't so easy, although everyone concerned had noticed and we were trying our best to keep things running smoothly.

I think it was day seven when we arrived at the studio to be told that Russ had gone home, and the project was suspended for the time being, although sadly we never did get back together again to complete things.

Russ's father had died a couple of weeks before we began the sessions, and it was understandably just too much for him to return to work so soon.

Home again, a bonus with regard to the recent improvements at Livingston was that I had a new project ready that I could bring to the studio right away.

I had been contacted by the guys who were about to become the new JV Band just prior to the Argent offer coming to me.

Pete (Biff) Byford and Paul Quinn were now in a band called Son Of A Bitch, and they had asked me to come and see them play with a view to helping them get a record deal.

They were playing at the Fforde Greene in Leeds, which had now become the go-to venue in town if you wanted some heavy rock, so I drove up there to witness a full-house with the band tearing the place apart, it was amazing!

It was clear to me that they had a future, so I agreed to get involved, and we booked some time at demo studios in London and proceeded to get some ideas down to play to record companies.

The band also needed management, so I invited my manager Dave Thomas to come and have a look — he also agreed that they really had something, and they were offered a management deal with Trident, which was duly signed and sealed.

With the demos completed, record labels were approached and pretty soon there was interest from EMI Records, but the head of A&R who liked the band was about to leave EMI and form his own setup.

After a short delay, Son Of A Bitch signed to this new label, Carrere Records owned by Frenchman Claud Carrere, with A&R covered by Peter Hinton who had also been at EMI.

We went into Livingston to record the album for real, but not before alarm bells began to ring. First of all despite the fact that I was managed by Trident I was put under pressure by them to change the direction of the band slightly, to try to cater for the American market, although our original demos were really straight ahead rock, more in the UK/European mould.

I really didn't want to do this, effectively take a little of the edge off the band's approach but was pushed that this was the way to go. Looking back, I should have dug my heels in, but hindsight is pointless, isn't it?

The next shock to me was that Carrere wanted to change the name of the band to Saxon, and I absolutely hated it. But what do I know.

Anyway, we got on with the album, sessions progressed pretty well although I did feel a bit of an atmosphere at times, I just tried to be professional about it.

Any band's first albums are tricky, as often they aren't quite rounded yet, and not all the material available might be suited to be included on an album, although absolutely fine in a band's live show.

The lineup of the band was Pete (Biff) Byford on lead vocals, Pete Gill on drums, Graham Oliver and Paul Quinn on guitars and Steve Dawson on bass.

When they first came to me as Son Of A Bitch, Biff played bass alongside Steve, but it sounded really messy and I suggested that Biff should stop playing bass and concentrate on being a front man, I believed it would suit the image of the band and they all agreed.

When I presented the first mixes to Carrere, they didn't like it. I didn't like it either but after some to-ing and fro-ing a final mix was agreed, although I still wasn't happy, and the album was released.

Despite my trying to do the best for the band under the circumstances, I've been the target of some unpleasantries over the years, however I have remained friends with Graham and Steve, and to a lesser extent with Paul.

Pete and I met again in 1983 when I produced some Motörhead stuff — he was playing drums with them at the time, and we got on just fine.

Our house in London had a long, fairly steep driveway from the front door up to the main road, and we had just had an unexpected snowfall in early 1979, things were quiet, there wasn't a great deal of traffic due to the weather conditions and I was surprised to hear the doorbell ring.

With the Saxon album finished, I was spending a little time at home in my studio, when the doorbell rang.

On answering the door, I was surprised to see a fourteen-year-old me looking back at me!

My son Ian had found me. A bit like me finding my sister Ella at a similar age, Ian had somehow found my address, and was now standing at my door saying "hello, I think you're my dad".

After too many years, this was the start of our relationship proper, and I'm glad to say that we are really close today, in regular contact although we're in different parts of the country, Ian, who is an accomplished bassist has even played with my band on a number of occasions.

Sadly, now suffering from Multiple Sclerosis, Ian is still living in the Bradford area, with his amazing wife Wendy, and I visit whenever I can.

Ian has three children, Ryan, Justine and Kimberly, with grandchildren Oliver, Nicky and Alessa, and Chase.

The Phoenix Rocket single, 'Time of the Season' was released around this time, but despite some cursory promotion by the label, didn't really take off and they seemed to abandon it quite quickly, ending our relationship with Rocket before it had really started.

Several meetings at the offices of our management later we decided to simply regroup, scrap the current album, and start again, beginning sessions to record the stuff that Ray and I had been writing at my place, where I still had a very basic demo setup.

Around this time, there was a really negative vibe around the established music scene in London, and we were simply out of fashion as a band — a group of musical Dinosaurs!

I insisted that we leave the country to record this new album, preferably to New York, where I felt there might be the energy to push us forward to making some really fresh-sounding stuff, and with a new deal with Charisma Records on the cards the decision was made to go for it.

Management told us that Roy Thomas Baker, who had produced much of the early successful Queen material, was really interested in producing us, and as I wanted to step back from producing the band to concentrate on my performances, I agreed it was a great idea.

A few days later we were told the studios were booked and our flights to L.A. were confirmed.

L.A? I'd said New York but was told that RTB (Roy Thomas Baker) was based at the Record Plant Studios in L.A. and wanted to work there.

His protégé, Stuart Alan Love was meeting us at S.I.R Studios, a rehearsal complex to routine the tracks for a week before we commenced sessions at Kendon Studios, and Record Plant to record what would eventually be the *In Full View* album.

So far, so bad, I hadn't wanted to work in L.A. as I really didn't want any risk of the sessions becoming laid-back in any way, and we still hadn't hooked up with RTB to make a valid plan and choose the actual material to be recorded.

It turned out his protégé was doing this part, apparently, and it all seemed a bit weird to me, although S.I.R was an interesting setup, and Thin Lizzy were in one of the other rehearsal studios where we were invited to call in and say hi/have a listen.

They were sounding great, with Gary Moore absolutely knocking it out of the park and we returned to our chores in our own rehearsal room feeling intimidated yet refreshed.

I was playing bass as we routined the songs, as we didn't feel ready to replace Jim yet, so I had opted to play bass on the basic tracks and put my guitars on later, once we had a good sounding track from the three of us.

These sessions weren't going well as we really didn't have a rapport with Stuart although he was trying hard to make it work.

RTB never did appear, and we began the actual recording sessions under the guidance of Stuart, and the house engineer Michael Boshears.

I wasn't happy, it wasn't sounding right, the atmosphere, as I had feared was far too laid back and we weren't being pushed to deliver our best.

I felt we were wasting an awful lot of time and money but by the same token I didn't want to be the one to break things up so I soldiered on as best I could, hoping we could fix it later, which of course is stupid.

The focus wasn't 100% on the music, one day early in proceedings the phone rang in the control room and Michael the engineer answered it, turning to us to say, "it's 'the Man' what does everyone want?"

It was obviously the local friendly drug dealer delivery person calling to see what we wanted — and of course we thought it was wonderful, asked what he had to offer and placed our orders. It went downhill from there.

As I said earlier, I had stepped back from the producer's role because I wanted to focus on my playing/singing, and I had also avoided letting anyone know that I was an engineer, but it became too much as I saw things progressing, or not.

I began to get involved in the production and tried also to rectify some of the stuff going on with regards to sound as I had really hoped for a more aggressive approach and Michael clearly didn't see it like that.

Regardless of the quality of the people involved to help us, and the quality of the studios we were working in I was very aware that we were signed to a UK record label being assaulted by Punk at the moment and they really wouldn't be happy if they could hear what we were putting down.

This was compounded when we received mock-ups for the album cover using photos that had been taken in L.A. with us looking like suntanned rock stars — like the archetypal LA rock royalty that the current UK record buyer despised, and of course Charisma hated the ideas.

Dave Thomas was with us in L.A., representing our management and one evening after our day in the studio I met with him and said I thought we should go home, as this just wasn't working. "Thank fuck for that" was his reply, he'd been seriously worried about the way it was going but didn't want to step in yet just in case we were able to pull it off somehow.

So, the sessions were cancelled, we bade our farewells and headed for the airport loaded down with boxes of 2" tape containing our work so far, hoping we could somehow salvage a viable album out of what we had recorded so far.

A few days after getting home I went into Trident Studios to listen to what we had, hoping that, with fresh ears I could work out where to go next, but what I was hearing just compounded all my fears, it just sounded weak and tired, and our L.A experiment had failed.

Time to book some time at my favourite studio, Livingston, and attempt to get *In Full View* fit for the current market, but first I had a session in the diary.

Chris White had been asked to produce a couple of established British acts and wanted to get Bob, Jim and I to provide the tracks.

Both projects were to be recorded at the 'Bronze' Roundhouse Studios in Chalk Farm, North London, with material a little out of our current comfort zone meaning we had to delve into our past to make it work.

Chris is a very kind, patient person and was happy to spend a little time whilst we 'got in the groove' for the stuff we had to play and pretty soon we had some nice tracks for the artist to sing to.

The first act was Diana Dors, the sixties film star who was still an extremely popular celebrity in the UK, mainly through TV appearances.

Diana was lovely to work with, no airs and graces, and these went by easily with the required single in the bag in double quick time.

Next up was Marti Caine, another popular TV celebrity, and these sessions went just as smoothly, again with us delving into our musical past to get the right feel for the songs.

Once these sessions had been completed it was time to get back to Phoenix.

Arrangements had already been made for Stuart Alan Love to travel to London to work on the tapes with me, and management didn't want to change that, so I went ahead and booked some time at Livingston Studios to allow us to work together.

Stuart arrived, but I made it clear that I had a plan and was taking the lead on finishing off the project, which I guess made him feel uncomfortable and as a result he didn't stay for long at all.

I invited Rod Argent to add some keyboard parts, and we had a sax part replaced, Russ Ballard did some backing vocals with me, and Ray and I spruced up our guitar parts, then finally I mixed the album as best I could.

After Stuart had gone, I also came to another conclusion — we didn't have a viable single on the album although Charisma wanted to go ahead and release it as it was, against my advice, and simply promote it as an album package.

We shot new cover photos in a style that Charisma thought was right for the UK market, *In Full View* came out in 1979 and Ray, Bob and I waited to see what would happen.

We were still bass player-less and invited a friend John Gordon to rehearse with us at my house in London. John had a great track record having played with lots of people including Alan Price, Bill Haley, Bernie Marsden, and the GB Blues Company which Bob was also a part of, meaning Bob was keen to have John G on board.

The rehearsals went really well and were timely as we'd just been booked to do a BBC Radio session at Maida Vale Studios to promote the album. I invited Rod Argent to join us on the day, as the tracks we were doing had keyboard parts that I thought were essential, and the recordings had to be 'live' i.e., nothing could be overdubbed or added.

It was great to play together as a band, despite the usual BBC hang-ups (don't get me started) and I have fond memories of that time.

Sadly, in the end not a lot happened with *In Full View* although Charisma still seemed to be onboard so I suggested we get a single out as soon as possible in the hope that we could promote the Phoenix name and create some interest in the catalogue as a whole, including *In Full View*.

Charisma agreed, but Ray and I didn't have any new material that was commercial enough for a single — however I knew who might have, so made a quick call to Russ Ballard to see if he had any new material that he would be prepared to give to Phoenix.

Russ said he'd love to help but didn't have anything finished to send to me — however if I wanted to meet, he could play me a few things on the piano to choose from.

I made my way to meet Russ at his place and he began playing me some ideas on piano, all interesting but not really what I was looking for, until one particular song was sounding nice, and then when he hit the chorus, "I Surrender, I Surrender" yes!! That's the one!

Russ played another couple of songs, and I chose another one to try, 'Juliet', before confirming with Russ that he would be okay to join us at Livingston Studios to record Juliet, and 'I Surrender' for Phoenix, as soon as possible.

Bob and Ray both agreed that the songs were strong, and we sketched them out together before meeting Russ at the studio to lay the tracks down, with Russ Playing piano, Bob on drums, Ray on guitar, and I think Dave Wintour on bass. Dave was a respected session guy at the time and had played lots of sessions for Russ and me recently.

I added my guitar parts later, as I often did.

We were all happy with the results, although 'I Surrender' was clearly the strongest, so I did rough mixes and arranged to take them into Charisma to choose the single.

Changes were afoot at Charisma Records, and the man responsible for establishing the label, and to a large extent choosing the most successful acts signed to it, Tony Stratton-Smith had gone.

I played my mixes to the new people, and they instantly didn't like 'I Surrender'.

"Not very commercial" was the response, and they "Weren't sure" about 'Juliet' but would "give it a try".

I was crestfallen, angry, and disgusted, 'I Surrender' was an obvious hit single in my opinion, and I know that the band and our management agreed.

There was nothing I could do, I had to call Russ and give him the bad news, and as a gesture, offer to give him our recording of

'I Surrender' to use as a demo to send to any bands who might be interested in recording it.

Ritchie Blackmore's band Rainbow received our demo, worked on it, and had a number three chart hit in 1980 with the song that I had hoped would save Phoenix. In the same year Charisma released our version of 'Juliet', with a section edited out of it because they didn't like it and it got precisely nowhere.

The situation with Ray had soured in recent times and our management were getting twitchy about what to do about it, although I couldn't really work out what was going on.

I think Ray had had meetings with them, but I wasn't sure what it was all about, but anyway the upshot was that we asked Ray to leave Phoenix.

I never really did get to the bottom of it, but it was a sad situation to be in especially considering our difficulties with Charisma.

Phoenix was now officially just me and Bob, although management had a plan it seems...

Before we departed from Charisma, I recorded a light-hearted version of 'Do You Love Me', originally recorded by The Contours, with Bob playing drums and Russ playing electric piano.

I did it as a joke and convinced the new people at Charisma that it was new young band I'd found called 'The Juniors'.

I received a nice advance which I shared with the guys before admitting to Charisma who it really was.

It was released as a single with one of my songs 'Babylon' on the B-side, in 1980.

To round off 1980 I sang on yet another Colin Blunstone album *Late Nights In Soho*, this time produced by Rod Argent, as always, a lovely project to be involved in with people I love and respect. Smiles all round.

14
More Ch-Ch- Changes!

Trident also managed a band called Charlie, who had had some success in America with their earlier albums but had been unable to break out really big.

It was suggested that they wanted to bring me in to help them record their next album, probably at Livingston Studios because I felt at home there and I was already getting the sort of sound they felt was needed to take them forward.

Terry Thomas was the leader of the band and wrote all the material — very fine material as it happens so I said yes right away, looking forward to getting started.

We booked a nice big block of time at Livingston and made a start on the album that would eventually be called *Good Morning America*.

It became clear to me pretty soon that Charlie's drummer Steve Gadd might not be able to get the very best out of all the material, and I suggested Bob Henrit came in to help. Everyone agreed surprisingly easily, even Steve, so I asked Bob to join us, and we got on with recording the basic tracks with Bob playing drums on the bulk of the songs and Steve doing the ones he felt most comfortable with. It was working really well.

The bands bassist John Anderson also agreed to step down for some of the songs so that Felix Krish, a well-respected session bassist could step in, and finally we hired Richard Cottle, a session keyboard player to add the 'fairy dust'.

I thought that was it, everything in place until one day when Terry approached me to ask me how I would feel about joining the band on lead vocals, and also provide some of the rockier guitar parts.

Finally, Dave Thomas, who was representing both Phoenix and Charlie in a management sense asked to meet with Bob and me and asked how we would feel about amalgamating Phoenix and Charlie to form a new band.

Bob and I agreed it would be a good idea, as we were going to have to regroup and find new people if we were to continue Phoenix, a bit of a no-brainer really as we were all getting on, and the stuff we were recording was sounding great.

So, we got on with the task in hand and made some excellent noises in the studio, which developed into strong finished product — despite too many trips to the pub, to sample the very strong beer on tap there!

All seemed to be going well although I was a bit taken aback when it was suggested the 'new' band should be called Charlie — I didn't think that was the plan, but what the hell did it really matter?

As time went on it did matter to me, and the sessions dragged on with a lot of the spontaneous elements swamped by what I felt was too much 'painting by numbers.'

I had envisaged a raw sound compared to earlier Charlie product and we seemed to be gradually slipping away from that which I found worrying and was turning me off the idea of this new band. I really felt that there was room for a more straight-ahead approach, and this wasn't it.

So, I announced that I was happy to complete and mix the album but that I wouldn't be staying, instead I was going to set out on a solo career in charge of my own destiny.

Good Morning America was released in 1981 and Charlie asked an excellent vocalist, Terry Slesser to replace me.

We didn't really part as friends, it was clear to me that they didn't really think I'd get anywhere as a solo artist, but I had a plan of my own...

Bob and I were still okay, and I invited him to come and do some sessions at Livingston, just the two of us with me in the control room playing guitar, singing, and engineering, with him in the studio live room rocking out in true Henrit style, much more like the Henrit I knew and loved. The drum parts I asked Bob to play were challenging — lots of tricky double-bass drum parts and flat-out power from start to finish.

I needed four strong tracks to take to record companies to try to get a deal and I knew exactly what I was looking for, no messing around, just straight between the eyes using strong material.

We recorded a version of 'You Keep Me Hanging On' first, then a full-on rock version of 'Day Tripper' followed by one of my favourite songs of all time 'Stay With Me Baby'.

The original version of 'Stay With Me Baby' was recorded by American artist Lorraine Ellison, and it had a huge orchestral arrangement, but I had always wondered if it would work as a rock song.

It was first released in 1966, but the real turning point for me was when the band I was playing guitar in, The Richard Kent Style, opened for Terry Reid, at Redcar Jazz Club in 1968, and he did his version of 'Stay with Me Baby'.

It absolutely blew my mind — this is it, it really can work outside the original approach, and the register of Terry Reid's voice was high, like mine, it was a real eureka moment, making me want to be a singer too.

So, all these years later I finally got around to recording it, in an even more straight-ahead version than Terry Reid's, but still keeping the essence of this amazing song.

As I sit writing this in 2023 it is only two days since I performed it at a show – Buxton Blues Festival where it still had the same impact as it had when I first performed it thirty years earlier! I love that song.

The final track that we recorded for my initial batch was Russ Ballard's 'Just Another Day (In The Life Of A Fool)', a track that we had recorded, I felt unsuccessfully, for the last Phoenix album in America, and it worked out much better this time.

I had just been offered a project to produce Brian Connolly, who had formerly been the lead singer of The Sweet, so I sent my first four tracks out to some prospective labels and focused on Brian's project for a while.

Brian was quite a character, but I soon had a soft spot for him as we worked at my place on possible material to record, and I also got on really well with his manager Don Alexander, a lovely, genuine bloke determined to help Brian rekindle his career.

I got the feeling that leaving The Sweet like he did had knocked Brian's confidence quite a bit, and he was struggling to focus once the time came to get into the studio and record the tracks we had chosen.

We had a really strong song, 'Hypnotized' to record for the 'A-side of a single, with one of Brian's own songs 'Fade Away' on the flip side.

A typical day would be Brian and his driver collecting me from home, and as we drove through Hampstead he would "need a loo" so we'd stop at a pub to use a toilet and of course it would be "let's have a quick drink" which turned into more until I began to get twitchy, insisting that we get to the studio. Brian was clearly trying to delay the start of our day in the studio.

I had recruited Bob Henrit to play drums and Dave Wintour to play bass, and we were recording at Livingston, so I was in my comfort zone in that sense, and there was soon a really nice atmosphere in the studio, helping to put Brian at ease.

With Bob and Dave in the studio and Brian providing a guide vocal, and me in the control room playing guitar and working the desk we soon had the basic tracks finished. Brian completed the vocal on 'Fade Away' pretty quickly, and I sang a huge bank of chorus vocals on 'Hypnotized' before sending Brian into the studio to complete a nice lead vocal.

Next, I added the rest of my guitar parts, asked my old friend Terry Uttley to add more vocal harmonies with me, and then did final mixes that we were all happy with.

Finally, I sent the mixes to Brian's label Carrere Records with trepidation bearing in mind my previous experience with them over the Saxon album.

No problem! All was well, the single was released in 1982 and Carrere asked me to put a band together to tour with Brian, opening for Pat Benatar who was in the UK at the time. I asked Bob Henrit and Terry Uttley to join me on drums and bass, with Terry and me providing the vocal harmonies that we had layered up on the recording of 'Hypnotized'.

Brian seemed really at home on stage, and the band gelled nicely, but there seemed to be little movement on the sales of 'Hypnotized' despite a really encouraging reaction from the audiences at our shows.

It didn't take long for Carrere to lose interest, and pretty soon things were at a standstill, and myself, Terry, and Bob really needed to get back to our own projects...

I tried to keep in touch with Brian, and my last meeting with him at a gig in the Northwest of England was a very sad affair, his health had really suffered, and the writing was on the wall I'm afraid.

Born on 5th October 1945, Brian sadly passed away on 10th February 1997.

It was time to focus on my own project, and with Don Alexander now involved we started to look at material to form a complete album.

Before I could get back to business though, I had a major upheaval on my hands to deal with as Pam and I were having problems, mostly of my making I admit, and we had agreed that a move back to Yorkshire might help to fix things between us and would be better for our kids, Ben, and Layla.

We had found a nice house in Cottingley, just outside Bradford, close to Pam's parents, and the house had ideal space to build a studio so perfect for everyone concerned under the circumstances.

We sold the house in London and made the move, found schools for the kids, built a new studio and then I proceeded to try and get a much-needed record deal to bring some money in.

I had explained to Don Alexander that although I had a number of my own songs written already, I was happy to record other people's songs if they were strong enough, and he agreed that that was a good idea so set about checking out what was available.

In the meantime, I was getting really nice feedback on the songs I'd sent out, and to my surprise was contacted by Mike Rutherford from Genesis saying he was really interested in producing me and had some songs he thought would work for me.

We arranged a meeting, and I explained that I was really enjoying producing the tracks myself and didn't want to change that, and luckily Mike said that was fine, and how about getting together to record his song ideas.

We worked out the details and I asked Bob to join me again, this time on a trip to Fisher Lane Farm, where Genesis had their studio, to work with Mike, on his songs.

We recorded three songs, and of these three I really felt that 'In The Arms Of Someone Else' was dead right for me and should be included on the album, so I took the tapes home to complete work on them in my new studio in Cottingley.

My old friend Geoff Lyth had thankfully stepped in to help me get the studio organised properly, and everything was sounding great.

Once I felt confident with the track, I invited Mike to join me at home, booked him into a nice hotel nearby and played him what I had done.

Mike seemed happy with it, and I assured him that I would use the other songs, but not on this album. He was okay with this.

I had completed a number of tracks at Livingston before the move to Yorkshire but still had more to complete and had made a start when there was a development.

There were three record deals on the table, all similar in terms of finance and I was still not decided on which one to go for when a deciding factor emerged.

Greg Lake from Emerson, Lake and Palmer had contacted me to say he had heard the four tracks and loved them enough to want them on the new record label that he was putting together. He offered me some session work too, and we spent a bit of time together — although I had been warned not to make it known to Keith Emerson, who I had worked with recently, as they weren't getting on at that time.

Coincidentally only a few weeks earlier, I had been contacted by Keith Emerson because he wanted me to sing and play on a project he was working on.

Keith had a contract with US film company Lorimar to provide music for their movies, and he wanted me to get involved in something he was currently working on, an as yet un-named Western.

The sessions would last about a week, and we would be working at his home in East Sussex where he had a large music/rehearsal/studio area in a large barn that also housed his iconic Yamaha keyboard setup.

Drummer Ainsley Dunbar was also there, playing on the sessions, but I can't remember the bassist's name although we all got on well, both in the studio and socially.

As it was for a movie, we worked in front of a huge screen, watching relevant sections of the film so we could sync our playing to the visuals when needed, although we also recorded the theme tune (which I sang), in the normal way that we would record a music track.

Keith would usually play acoustic piano when we were laying the tracks down, I guess he would have intended to add other keyboard parts once we had gone.

The sessions went well enough, although Keith seemed 'troubled' much of the time.
The rest of us just tried to be professional and gave the best we could to the situation.

I don't know if the movie was ever released, it seemed like a pretty epic project, but I lost contact with Keith after this one.

Keith died of a self-inflicted gunshot wound on 11th March 2016 at his home in Santa Monica, California. R.I.P Keith Emerson, one of the finest keyboard players in the business.

On the album front, I had also had an offer from RCA Records, but the one that really had me excited was from, of all labels PRT, formally

Pye Records who had a very varied catalogue from The Kinks to Max Bygraves.

The reason for my interest in PRT was the head of A&R, Matt Haywood, because of his enthusiasm and obvious deep knowledge of the industry, including my kind of music.

Matt really did seem interested in what I had to offer, and I really felt we could have a great, lasting relationship.

A contract was sent for me to check out — a very old-school contract with lots of what I considered to be outdated clauses, so I went about crossing things out before sending it back to PRT, awaiting the word to attend PRT offices for the official signing (and collecting of the cheque).

I think I must have got a bit carried away with my 'crossing out' because Matt looked a bit surprised when I returned to his office but said, "Okay can you pop along to see the Old Man, he'll take it from here".

I was a bit taken aback at having to meet the 'Big Cheese' but was led to huge office by a very mature secretary to the MD to finalise things. And to meet Walter Woyda.

On entering the room, I was greeted by an elderly man, the Managing Director, who, on seeing me began to gesticulate and shout, "how dare you ask for such changes to our standard contract, this is ridiculous!"

I held my ground and explained, very politely that I felt that a lot of what was in contract originally was outdated and not really appropriate in today's market.

This seemed to calm him down a bit and the atmosphere lightened up, he pushed the contract towards me on the desk, we both signed, shook hands and I left.

The Secretary handed me the cheque as I left Mr Woyda's office and returned to a laughing Matt Haywood in his office — the start of a lifelong friendship (you bastard!).

The clauses I had removed?

Well, there was some obvious old-fashioned stuff like the company having the right to tell me how to behave in public, and what to wear in public.

But the main thing that I think he didn't like was that I had removed the right for the label to recoup certain things from my royalties, for example since I had moved back to Yorkshire there were many trips to

London required, with travel expenses and stays in expensive hotels to pay for. I wanted them to pay, and not take the money from my royalties.

There would also be tour expenses, and again I expected them to pick up the bill and not deduct it from my future earnings.

Anyway, it all turned out fine in the end, but I think in hindsight I was very lucky to get away with it.

Now to the business in hand, with the contact signed I now had access to PRT Studios, formerly Pye Studios, ATV House, Great Cumberland Place, just off Marble Arch, London.

There were two studios there, Studio One was probably unchanged from the sixties, with a beautiful Neve console a bit like the one at Livingston, and a huge live room to record the tracks — perfect for drums.

Studio Two was more of a remix room, with a very complex 'Cadac' console and much more modern design and resources — not really what I was looking for as I was going to mix at home in Cottingley.

I set about organising musicians for the final sessions for what would become my *Interrupted Journey* album, although there was one complication to overcome when I got the news that Bob had been offered a great new opportunity.

He had been recording on a solo album by Dave Davies of The Kinks, as a session player, and as a result came to the attention of brother Ray who of course was impressed, leading to an offer to join The Kinks alongside our old friend Jim Rodford.

It was a fantastic opportunity for Bob, but it meant that he would be far too busy to complete *Interrupted Journey* with me and I needed to find a new drummer, double quick!

As it happens, the solution was pretty close to home, as I was already aware that Jim's son Steve was a rapidly developing drummer, very much in the Henrit mould.

These days Steve has a style of his own, he is the drummer in the current lineup of The Zombies, alongside Rod Argent, and Colin Blunstone but back then his style was very influenced by Bob as he had grown up watching him playing alongside his dad in Argent.

I approached Steve and asked him to join me in recording the final album tracks, followed by a UK and European tour, and he accepted. He would be playing alongside my old mate Terry Uttley on bass, from the band Smokie, who was already recording with me at the time.

I wanted another guitarist in the touring band too and we asked Steve's friend John Willoughby, who was in Steve's own band at the time — I'd done some recording with them at Livingston a few months earlier. John said yes and we were pretty much sorted.

There was a small diversion at this point before I could get home to carry on with my album, when Matt Haywood asked me if I would produce some tracks with The Searchers, the successful sixties band who had originally been signed to Pye Records, and now with PRT.
I said yes right away, eager to hear what they sounded like these days, as their last album had been a minor success in America and was hoping to build on that.

On listening to the demo tapes Matt sent over to me at the hotel I could immediately hear a weak link, as the current drummer, not an original member of the band didn't have the 'feel' I was hoping to get on the tracks.

A quick call to Bob Henrit and I was able to grab him for a couple of days recording at PRT Studios before he went off on tour with The Kinks, and we laid the basic Searchers tracks down successfully with the intention of finishing them at home later.

For the remaining couple of days at PRT Studios, Steve, and I along with Terry completed the rest of the basic tracks for *Interrupted Journey* and I took the tapes home to Cottingley to fine tune everything and do the mixing.

First of all, I added my own guitar parts — we had only put a rough 'guide' guitar down at PRT Studios, along with a guide vocal as I was only really concerned with getting a great drum performance for each song, with the bonus of a great bass part at the same time. Everything else could wait until we got home.

I completed all my guitar parts, worked on my lead vocals and then Terry and I put together some strong vocal harmony parts. The track 'Rescue Me' was sounding very strong — a possible single already, which was a great relief.

It became obvious that the new tracks needed some keyboards at this point, and although Rod Argent, with contributions from Andy Clark and Richard Cottle, all based in London or thereabouts, had been playing the keyboard parts for me at Livingston, I didn't feel I could drag them all the way up to Yorkshire to do the rest.

I had used a local keyboardist Dave Cass at the Cottingley studio but the keyboard parts we needed were quite basic, just to add a little colour to the overall sound and it turned out that there was someone quite local to us who could do the job for us.

Andy Tidswell was based nearby, and available so he joined us for the final recordings, and part of the upcoming tour.

As an artist, I had been off the scene for a while so in order to promote the album properly I needed to be prepared to tour in an opening slot to a major band.

By now, Saxon had reached this status, and were planning to go out on the road to promote their latest album, so PRT approached them, proposing me as the support act on this tour, and the offer was accepted.

The tour was to cover the UK, Europe and Scandinavia so it was an ideal opportunity to get to lots of people with *Interrupted Journey* and hopefully generate some sales and raise the profile of the band, which I had simply called Verity.

We rehearsed, and the band was sounding really tight as the tour start date approached I felt really happy and confident we would make a good impression on the tour, hoping the atmosphere between me and the Saxon guys would be okay.

As we began the tour, it soon became clear the everyone was going to behave in a professional manner, although I did detect problems in the Saxon camp.

Saxon had just released their *Crusader* album and I remember that at one show our dressing room was in a kitchen area where there were lots of aluminium cooking utensils, perfect for dressing up as a crusader, with pans for helmets, trays for a shield and huge knives for a sword.

I burst into Saxon's changing room dressed as a crusader, using the stuff I'd found in our changing room, to find that they were in the middle of some sort of altercation — my timing wasn't great that day!

The tour was going really well, and we had a great reception wherever we went but then suddenly I had to deal with a hiccup with the band which started one morning when I walked into the hotel breakfast room to find Andy sitting there looking upset.

I sat with him, and he told me he had just heard that his grandmother, who he was really close to, had suddenly died. I could see how upset he was, so I offered to buy his plane ticket to get him home for the funeral, saying that we could manage without keyboards for the next stretch of the tour.

Andy thanked me, but said he's rather stay and see the tour through to the end.

I hoped that everything would be okay but a few days later the same thing happened, apparently Andy had had the awful news that his grandad had now passed away and he wanted to accept my offer of a flight home.

Andy left right away.

We completed the tour successfully without keyboards, and on our return home I decided to try to, discretely find out how Andy was doing, I knew his sister ran a pub in nearby Bingley, so I called into see her, and said how sorry I was to hear about her grandparents.

I won't repeat what she actually said, but let's say she was shocked to hear this; I think they were actually alive and well...

Things were looking good with *Interrupted Journey*, with decent reviews, an immediate leap into the *Kerrang!* magazine chart and respectable sales so far plus I already had ideas for a follow-up album so was keen to get back into the studio.

A side effect of the publicity was I was being offered production work with some of the heavier acts on the scene, but first I need to make some improvements to the studio.

Part of the plan for the move to Yorkshire involved raising money from my shares in Livingston Studios.

Jerry Boys, an acclaimed sound engineer and producer had been booking time at Livingston, and like me was really impressed — impressed enough to want to get involved.

Jerry had ideas about 'improving' the studio that I didn't really agree with, such as dumping the lovely Neve consoles in favour of the new kid on the block at the time, SSL.

I saw this as an opportunity to get out and sign my shares over to Jerry therefore raising the funds, I needed to fully equip the studio at our new location. The deal went through, raising the cash in time to make the improvements I needed to move the new place forward.

I needed building work done at the new place, and we had a local painter and decorator, Billy Barton already working in our home above the studio, and as luck would have it Billy was in fact a craftsman who could do everything I needed downstairs too.

Building work completed, I asked my old friend Geoff Lyth to join me, first of all to finish the wiring and organising and then to help on sessions when he was free.

Geoff was to spend a lot of time with me over the next couple of years as we gradually improved things in the studio, and he also helped on the engineering front as well as providing writing and production ideas.

Geoff's diaries from our times in the JV band and these times in the studio have been invaluable when writing this book too — thank you Geoff!

Pretty soon everything was ready, and Tank arrived to record their album *This Means War*, which was a really good test of the new facilities. Tank were a full-on rock outfit capable of blowing the place apart! All went extremely well, I finished mixing the album, the label and band were happy and so was I. Result!

This Means War came out in 1983.

During the sessions for *This Means War* I met their manager Doug Smith and I guess he was impressed enough to keep me in mind for any future projects.

Doug also managed Motörhead who were due to start a short UK tour soon, and he approached me to see if I was interested in recording some of the shows for a possible live album, which of course I agreed to do.

We were going to be using the Rolling Stones Mobile truck for these recordings and as I approached the first venue which I believe was the Manchester Apollo, I could hear the band sound-checking in the venue.

I approached the truck, climbed up the steps leading to the control room to see that the engineer who travelled with the mobile had already got everything sorted out, and each channel of the recording console was nicely labelled with the instrument microphone being used.

I sat at the desk and pushed up the 'kick drum' mic. but was surprised to hear everything on it so I pulled down and tried the 'snare drum' mic., but that was the same.

I turned around and looked at the engineer and he just shrugged, so I climbed down the steps and headed for the stage to try and see what was wrong.

As I walked on stage the band were still playing and it was deafening! So loud in fact that the guitars and Lemmy's bass guitar were bleeding into the drum mics. Hence the problems in the control room.

Oh well, I'd just have to deal with it.

The band stopped playing, I said hi to everyone, then got back to the job in hand back in the truck trying to get it to sound right.

The band carried on sound-checking, and I was working on the sound when I was aware of someone behind me.

It was Doug Smith and at that point I was sure I'd be on my way home pretty soon as I was feeling that it really wasn't sounding so good, when suddenly Doug's voice rang out shouting "Fucking Great!"

Feeling a lot more confident, we went ahead and recorded the show, planning to go into a studio in Manchester the next day to see if anything needed fixing, and then to mix each song.

After fixing a few vocal bits, Lemmy said he was going to leave me to it, and as he headed for the door I called after him, "it'll sound great when I've added the backing vocals, man".

Lemmy turned to me and said, "do you wanna fucking die?".

I was joking of course, but I'm not sure Lemmy was...

The next album of this vein that I did was a band called Baby Tuckoo, who were located locally but had secured a decent record deal with an established label, Albion Records who seemed well organised and equipped to promote the band properly.

The finished album sounded great, and I really did think the band had a great future ahead but sadly it was not to be, as there didn't seem to be enough initial traction the get the label motivated to really get behind the project.

A single from the album was released — the bands version of the classic 'Mony, Mony' but to no avail so the project faltered. Such a shame.

During this period, I had a number of offers that I chose to turn down, preferring to focus on my own career rather that join someone else's band.

There were other reasons too of course, I had promised myself that from now on I wouldn't attempt to work with anyone I didn't like, or in situations where I felt uncomfortable, and with each of these offers came little 'red lights' warning me that this wasn't for me.

Ted Nugent's manager approached me at one point, to say that Ted wanted to get together to discuss the possibility of me joining his band, he was touring the UK at the time, so it seemed sensible to meet and discuss the options.

In the meantime, they had sent some recordings and asked me to add vocals to them, which I did at Livingston, and sent the mixes back to Ted's management.

Soon after that, Ted was playing at The Rainbow Theatre in London, and I was invited along to see the show, with a meeting planned the next day at a restaurant in town, to finalise details if I was to join Ted's Band.

The show was everything I'd expected, completely over the top — Ted is quite a character, and I couldn't really work out where I might fit in, but I attended the meeting the next day anyway, which was attended by Ted, his management, and people from his record label.

I knew right away that this wasn't going to work, it really wasn't the gig for me, but I felt cornered as it seemed to be assumed that I would do it.

Ted seemed keen to have me join him at his place in the US where we could 'kill stuff' — he preferred to kill the things he liked to eat.

Sometimes in situations like this I'm prone to doing something extreme, and this is what happened next; I was wearing a sweater with a T-shirt underneath, and I said to Ted that a new band seemed like a great idea, but we'd have to think of a name for the band.

With that I stood up and pulled up my sweater to reveal the John Verity Band T-Shirt underneath.

No-one laughed.

We finished our meal and I left, and of course there was no more discussion about JV joining Ted Nugent.

The next offer to emerge was with Michael Schenker, and again it didn't really seem up my street as there was little likelihood of me playing much guitar in his band.

Apparently, there were currently two singers in the band, Gary Barden who had been there for some time, and Derek St Holmes who also played guitar but was leaving the band to return home to the US.

I was intrigued and was sent some recordings to learn and asked to join Michael for a gig at Middlesborough Town Hall, the final show of his current UK tour, which I agreed to, not really knowing what to expect, except that I would join the band on stage to sing and play a few songs.

Steve Waite drove me up to Middlesborough on the day and we arrived in time for soundcheck at the venue, where amps were set up for me on the opposite side of the stage to Michael.

Pretty soon I noticed that there was a guitar tech sitting out of sight behind Michael's stacks of amps, playing guitar parts to compliment what Michael was doing. All good, but every now and again Michael would turn to give instructions to him, and it looked as if he was talking to his amps, which I found really funny, so I started talking to my amps.

The crew clearly found this situation hilarious, as lots of stifled chuckles could be heard as they spotted what was going on, but Michael wasn't amused and asked if we could have a word, explaining that this was his band and therefore the focus should be on him, not me.

Hmm this wasn't for me...

Incidentally, the opening band that night was Wildlife who had Simon Kirke on drums.

So showtime came, I went on at the allotted time and to my surprise Michael announced me as the new member of the band.

We played well together, and Michael was happy, and later at the hotel he asked to speak to me saying that he really thought it was going to be great having me in the band and there would be lots for me to do as he was going to 'get rid' of Gary Barden meaning I'd be doing all the singing.

We were sitting on a couch next to a low table, and sitting on the couch opposite was Gary Barden, clearly able to hear the conversation, this was awful and convinced me that this wasn't a situation I'd be happy being a part of.

I said nothing at the time, bade farewell to everyone, and Steve drove me home to Cottingley, where I frantically tried to get hold of Schenker's management to tell them I wouldn't be on the flight to the US on Sunday. I couldn't reach them, and the upshot is that for the first time I my career I just didn't turn up.

I think Schenker did the US tour with the lineup from the previous tour intact while they looked for someone to replace Derek St Holmes, although this wasn't my last encounter with Michael Schenker...

Some time later I had a call from Michael, he was working on a new album in his brother Rudy's studio and needed my help, could I fly out to Munich right away?

It sounded important, so I agreed to help, not really knowing what was going on but curious I guess. I was picked up at Munich airport and taken to Rudy's amazing studio — I think the only studio I've been to with an indoor swimming pool!

We listened to the tracks they had already recorded, and I began to lay down vocals but again I was uneasy about the situation, something wasn't right.

The next day I told Michael it wasn't for me and was going to leave, I was taken to the airport, back to London and that was the end of it.

Back home once again I was working in the studio when the phone rang, and I answered it to find I was talking to Ray Davies of The Kinks! Quite a shock as you can imagine, and even more surprisingly Ray was inviting me to join The Kinks, as apparently Dave Davies was about to leave the band.

At the end of our brief chat, Ray said someone would be in touch soon to arrange a rehearsal with the band, and he was looking forward to working together. I couldn't believe it! A few days later I did get a call, but not the one I was hoping for, as apparently Dave wasn't leaving the band after all, and it seemed I now wouldn't be needed.

Finally, to round off the year I was approached with a 'mystery' project!

I got a call to say a major band wanted me to join them for a tour of Japan, but it had to be kept quiet because changes in the lineup had not yet been announced.

I was asked to attend a rehearsal in Park Royal, London where all would be revealed.

I knew that Don Alexander had a rehearsal place in Park Royal so I called him to enquire who the mystery band was, but he said, "I can't tell you, it's a secret!" I knew he was winding me up, but I just gave in and got into the car to drive to Park Royal and find out for myself.

Some 'secret!' — piled high outside the rehearsal studio were dozens of flight cases bearing the legend 'ASIA'.

I walked into the studio, where they were rehearsing, and looking through the glass I could see that Greg Lake was playing bass. It seems he had been brought in to replace original bassist John Wetton and I'm guessing it was Greg who suggested me for the gig.

I also spotted guitarist Steve Howe, formerly of Yes, so it was clear they only wanted me for my voice, which of course was not going to happen. I'm a guitarist.

I stood there for a while, watching them play for a bit, argue for a bit, play for a bit more and argue for a bit more, and so on, it wasn't a happy ship, and definitely not my cup of tea as it was getting quite nasty, so I left.

A little later I got a call from them again, suggesting that if I would agree to do the tour I could bring a friend with me, possibly to do some backing vocals and keep me company. I didn't really fancy that, but I mentioned it to my friend Terry Uttley to see if he was interested but he wasn't, so I declined the offer.

Whilst all this was going on, my friend Chris White was spending quite a bit of time in the studio with me as we worked on his 'Software Girl' project, that you could probably call an early Sci-Fi idea meant for the stage, but with an accompanying album.

Words and music for the project were by Chris and his close friend Patrick Williams, and as ever Chris brought along amazing material, and people to put together some wonderful moments in the studio.

Sadly, 'Software Girl' never did make it to the stage, but it remains one of the most interesting projects I've ever worked on and was my introduction to one of the most talented musicians I have ever worked with, Sebastian Santa Maria.

Sebastian was a Chilean-Swiss musician and composer who Chris met in Lausanne through mutual friends, and although it looked as if he had a bright future ahead, he sadly died due to developing Adrenoleukodystrophy, a disease that affects the nervous system, in October 1996. R.I.P Sebastian you were a musical genius.

This Rock 'n' Roll Won't Last You Know!

15
Friends

As a side project, Terry, and I together with Alan Silson and Pete Spencer, also from Smokie decided to put a band together, partly for a bit of fun but also with the aim of raising money for charity. We called the band The Hooligans and left it to Steve Waite to get us a few gigs for our project while our loosely termed rehearsals took place.

Much of our rehearsal time was spent in the pub, making a list of songs we might do and in fact I don't think we actually did any rehearsing, preferring instead to just 'wing it' at the gig, and it really seemed to work. Chaotic, but good fun, and The Hooligans even managed to record a version of 'The Locomotion' before we all drifted back to our regular projects again.

It was great fun while it lasted, and a welcome diversion from our regular projects, I certainly think I needed it at that time, considering the uncertainty of my own situation.

So, it was now 1984, and I was deep into discussions with PRT about where to go with my career with them, leading to regular trips to London for meetings.

After a day of meetings, I would usually stay at the Montcalm hotel in London, and Matt Haywood and I would often meet there afterwards for a drink in the bar.

One evening as we sat drinking, Matt in particularly good mood after far too many drinks began to annoy other drinkers by being a bit loud, although the banter was very good natured.

A member of staff came over and asked Matt to leave, whereby Matt angrily waved his car keys and headed for the door, closely followed by me trying to relieve him of the car keys and put him in a cab.

Matt was having none of it and began to get shirty with me so I turned and walked back into the bar, but before I could take my seat, I could hear a roar of an engine outside followed by a screech of tyres and a loud bang.

I ran outside to see Matt's car upside down in the middle of the road, with Matt trying to get out through one of the broken windows, he hadn't seen the skip parked down the street from his parking space and had hit it at high-speed resulting in this mess.

I think Matt left the scene of the accident despite his injuries, but to be honest it's all a bit of a blur.

Soon after, Matt announced his departure from PRT, I think he had been unhappy there after all and had plans to form his own company, but for now it meant changes afoot at PRT that might not be to my liking.

Robin Blanchflower became head of A&R at PRT, having spent successful years at A&M Records in the U.S. At my first meeting with Robin, I played him a track I had just recorded, a song recommended to me by Terry Uttley, 'What About Me', a cover of the song first released by Australian band Moving Pictures.

My version of the song was a bit of an over-the-top production I admit but I was aiming for the singles market and thought it might work, and so did Robin. His enthusiasm as I played the track to him in his office surprised me, and delighted me at the same, maybe my apprehension about the changes at PRT were unfounded?

The single came out in the UK and Europe, creating enough attention for Terry and me to do some promotional TV shows but it wasn't a hit record as we had hoped so it was back to the drawing board.

Mum & Dad

Dad with his cornet

Grange Boys Grammar School

Dad and Mum at the seaside

Dad, Mum, me & brother Paul

GM Pip – with Ian front left

Me with my first Stratocaster

THE RICHARD KENT STYLE

The Richard Kent Style 1968

Me with my Les Paul, Kent Style days

Harvey Starr aka Dick Kent, Kent Style days

Dave Bowker, Kent Style saxophonist

Me at Jokers Wild

Jokers Wild Club, 1969

'Tunnel', Freeport, Grand Bahama

Harvey Rose, bassist extraordinaire, Jokers Wild

Alby Greenhalsh aka Alby Bear, Jokers Wild

Me on my private beach! Freeport, Grand Bahama

Second JV Band UK Lineup, Geoff Lyth and Barry at the back Rowland Dawson and me at the front

Third JV Band lineup, Geoff Lyth, Gerry Smith, Ron Kelly & Me

First UK JV Band bassist, Mally Siswick

At Mum and Dad's house, John Street, Wakefield, 1972

Geoff Lyth, guitarist,
and friend extraordinaire!

First JV record deal signing, Mel Collins (Manager), Me, Dave Chapman (Probe Records), & Steve Rowland (Producer)

Argent Mk II, Bob Henrit, Jim Rodford, Me, Rod, John Grimaldi

Me at the Marquee Club, Wardour Street, London 1974

My favourite Phoenix shot, Bob Henrit, Me & Jim Rodford

My Band, promoting 'Interrupted Journey', on Ilkley Moor. baht 'at

Terry Uttley R.I.P.

Israel Cottage, Nr Clapham North Yorkshire

Steve Thompson & 'Gus'

Terry Swain, Me & Brian West, with Craig Ellis on drums out of sight

The Diesel Band, Jilly's legs, JC and me at the back, with Jeff Brown & Ray Minhinnett at the front

JV Band drummer and very fine chap

Jamie Mallender, JV Band Hippy bassist

Roger Inniss, a very fine bassist and wonderful fellow

My little Piranha Fish, lovely Carole and me on our wedding day

Carole, wrapped up in the cold

Liam James Gray, makin' a racket behind me

John Gordon, all round brilliant chap and bassist

Steve, with Jim Rodford R.I.P.

Me, doing my thing...

Bassist and promoter, Derek White

Another extraordinary bassist and brilliant fellow, Mr Bob Skeat

Carole & Wendy

The Geezers

JV Band & Verity Bromham drummer Chris Mansbridge doing his stuff

Verity Bromham & Stray bassist Colin 'Curvy' Kempster

A very sweaty Verity Bromham Band

Soul brother Del, with me at the back

16
Into The Future...

Before his departure, Matt had introduced me to songwriter Steve Thomson, an eccentric Geordie songsmith with great ideas that seemed to fit with mine. Steve came down to the studio in Cottingley and we hit it off straight away, slipping into a routine for working together that would for some time produce some really good material.

As well as being a writer, Steve was also an excellent bassist, played keyboards well and had already got a good grasp of the new technology that allowed computers to be used as tools in the studio.

At the time I was strictly analogue, but this mix of technology and attitudes somehow seemed to work, and we got down to creating some really interesting stuff from day one of our partnership.

Steve also liked a drink, and at that time in my life I know I was drinking far too much, with the added danger that it didn't seem to affect my work, and no-one ever seemed to notice, or comment either in the studio or when we were socialising.

I'm sure Pam must have hated it too, but nothing was ever said...

So, we embarked on long days/nights in the studio with regular trips down to the pub, churning out ideas that turned into finished product for what would eventually be my next album, *Truth of the Matter*.

One time in the pub, I remarked to Steve that I thought you probably could put anything at all in the muzak/background music in the pub and no-one would notice.

He agreed, we went back to the studio and composed and recorded a thirty-minute piece to put on cassette and take back to the pub for them to play.

On our next visit we handed it over, they were delighted, accepted the cassette tape and often we would arrive at the pub for a break to hear our track 'Show Us Your Tits' playing in the background, with no-one noticing.

Looking back, it's obvious that Steve and I were really bad for each other, not in a songwriting sense as we wrote some really nice stuff together, but socially we were a nightmare. For example, Steve reminded me recently of an incident late one night when we were in the studio as usual and one of us remarked on our unhealthy lifestyle.

"We should go jogging, that's healthy".

So, we did go jogging that night in Cottingley. Naked.

Luckily, nobody saw us.

Truth of the Matter was released in 1985 with one of my favourite covers designed by Chess, a company run by Peter Lacy who became a good friend through the PRT period and beyond. The cover was very simple, mostly white but the main emblem was embossed, making it feel special, to me. Sadly Peter is no longer with us.

I felt the album was strong, the songs Steve and I had written combined with some of mine, and the contribution made by Geoff made for quite a varied but interesting feel throughout, from the full-on rock tracks to the more melodic ones, plus a couple of covers to round the whole thing off.

I had already recorded 'Roll The Dice' with Charlie but had never been happy with the finished article so I did my own version and included it here, alongside one of the tracks Mike Rutherford had written for me, 'Hold On To Love'.

Steve and I had agreed a 50/50 arrangement for songs we had written together, with my share on Verity Music, my own company, and Steve's credited to DJM Music who Steve had a publishing deal with.

I didn't expect any complications with this arrangement, but this wasn't quite true — more on this later…

A single, 'Honesty and Emotion' a Verity/Thompson composition, on both 7" and 12" format (we were still on vinyl) was released soon after the album, to a pretty luke-warm reception.

There didn't seem to be much going on in terms of promotion by PRT and felt the death-knell of our relationship was on the cards, but not before a major event rocked our lives.

17
The Fire

I had made my customary Friday trip to London for meetings, staying over at the Montcalm as usual and catching an early train back to Bradford when out of the taxi windows it became obvious that there was a major fire in town.

We reached Cottingley and I entered the house to see a horrifying scene on TV, the Bradford City football ground, Valley Parade was on fire.

Saturday 11th May 1985 was a grim day for the people of Bradford when during the home football match earlier that day a fire erupted, killing fifty-six spectators and injuring around two hundred and sixty-five.

Much of the stadium was constructed of wood, and the main stand had already been condemned although work to replace it with a steel structure hadn't commenced yet, leaving it vulnerable to the disaster happening that day.

The fire built rapidly, television presenter John Helm commented at 3:40 pm that there was a small fire in the main stand, and within four minutes the fire had engulfed the whole of that stand, trapping people in their seats, many burnt to death.

There were many cases of heroism with more than fifty people later receiving police awards for bravery for what they did on the day.

The people of Bradford were united in a way that I had never seen before, and the place was awash with charity events, raising money for survivors and charities.

Songwriter Graham Gouldman, of 10cc fame contacted many artists, including myself with a view to making a recording to raise money for a burns unit and I in turn recruited lots of my friends in the business to appear on the record, from Motörhead to Smokie, right across the musical spectrum.

We recorded a version of the Rogers and Hammerstein song 'You'll Never Walk Alone', due to it's obvious links with football and invited Gerry Marsden to sing lead vocals on the single.

We needed to work quickly, as the money was needed immediately, so I contacted Nick Kinsey who was still at Livingston to ask for some free time to record a B-side.

Nick said yes right away, and we decamped there to, hopefully, simply add some messages from famous people on top of the backing track from the B-side, using the phone line that Nick had connected to the mixing console to allow us to record the 'guests' remotely.

Best laid plans... the publishers of 'You'll Never Walk Alone' wanted a ridiculous amount of money to allow us to use the backing track so we declined and set about writing something for the messages to go on top of. A nice moving piece of music, not too intrusive so the spoken messages thanking those who had bought the single could be heard clearly.

Everyone we contacted, including Paul McCartney, contributed on the day as requested and we completed the single in double quick time with our B-side simply called 'Messages'.

It virtually came out overnight and was in the shops immediately, rising straight to number one on the 15th of June 1985 a little over a month after the fire broke the heart of the City of Bradford.

But it didn't break the spirit! Read on...

We called the band 'The Crowd' and its members were from right across the entertainment industry: Sir Bruce Forsyth, Denny Laine, Jim Diamond, Tony Christie, Rick Wakeman, John Conteh, The Barron Knights, Jess Conrad, Kiki Dee, The Foxes, Rolf Harris, Graham Gouldman, Kenny Lynch, Rick Wild of The Overlanders, Keith Chegwin, Tony Hicks, Colin Blunstone, Tim Hinkley, Johnny Logan, Zak Starkey, Girlschool, Black Lace, John Otway, Gary Holton, Peter Cook, the Nolans, John Entwistle of The Who, Motörhead, Dave Lee Travis, Graham Dene, Ed Stewart, Phil Lynott, Smokie, Joe Fagin, Eddie Hardin, Gerard Kenny, Tim Healy, Rose Marie, David Shilling, Chris Norman, Bernie Winters, Robert Heaton, and Frank Allen of The Searchers.

I had already, together with my tour manager Steve Waite, begun to set up a weekend of concerts at Bradford's St Georges Hall to raise funds for the burns unit.

My plan was to have three separately themed nights, Friday would be an alternative music night, Saturday a Pop music event and Sunday was Rock flavoured.

I was determined that 100% of the proceeds would go to the charity and that there would be zero expense, first approaching St Georges Hall to get them to agree to letting me have the three days/nights free of charge. They reluctantly, agreed.

Next, I approached a major company, Malcolm Hill to provide PA and lighting for all three nights, and it had to be free of charge, they agreed — and after our final show on Sunday went on to provide the same facilities for Live Aid.

The trucks with PA and lighting arrived on the Friday morning direct from a European tour, with full crew ready to set up for Friday's show featuring several local bands keen to help the cause.

In the meantime, I had approached several restaurants in the Bradford area to provide food for the crew, and artists backstage. Again it had to all be free of charge, and companies both large and small came forward with offers of help, it really was an amazing time with so many people keen to help, from every community in the city.

The two main hotels in the city centre provided accommodation for visiting artists, free of charge and finally I contacted the MD of British Rail who arranged for me to have access to travel cards, again free of charge for those needing to travel by train.

I persuaded Smokie to reform to headline the Saturday show and arranged for Gerry Marsden to make an appearance so we could close Saturday night's event with 'You'll Never Walk Alone', which had just taken the number one slot in the charts, with everyone from the earlier bands onstage all together for this.

For the Sunday show I got Argent back together, Rod, Jim, Bob and me, and persuaded Colin Blunstone to come and do a set as well. My band for our set on the Sunday evening was the same as for the Saxon tour, but with Steve Thompson on keyboards so it was nice and tight, and we served as the 'house band' if anyone needed us.

Fellow Bradfordian Kiki Dee was happy to come along too, with our 'house band' doing the honours, and I joined her onstage for support.

Baby Tuckoo had done an earlier set and there was lots of good music that night with old friends making a joyous racket together!

After it was all done, I was exhausted and I'm sure Steve Waite was too — I couldn't have done it without him.

100% of the money we made over the three nights went into the Bradford Disaster Fund.

18
Back To Reality

Music is amazing. I was in a very bad place at this time, but I doubt anyone would have noticed, many musicians seem to train themselves to separate their private lives from their work, and I guess I'm one of them.

The show must go on after all…

I was in a terrible mess financially, and my relationship with Pam was such that I didn't feel I could share the worry with her, it wasn't Pam's fault at all, but I was falling to pieces and really didn't know what to do about it.

I had a couple of projects coming up but nothing major and it was clear to me that PRT were about to drop me without taking up the option for a planned third album, although I really needed the money.

It was a disaster waiting to happen although I had had a meeting with Robin Blanchflower which seemed to suggest I may be wrong about the impending doom.

I wasn't thinking straight, and had convinced myself that it would be better if I walked out on Pam and the kids and keep them away from the problems for good, what was I thinking?

I was still making the Friday trips to London in the hope that I could pull something together and at times it looked like things might be okay, especially since my recent meetings at PRT.

Matt Haywood had, by now formed his own record label, Sierra Records and got back in touch with a project for Steve and me to write a song for Mike Pender, who had just left The Searchers to pursue a solo career, and we came up with 'It's Over' for his first release on Sierra.

Recording the A-side went well enough as Steve and I did everything, and Mike just had to come in and sing the lead vocal, which he did, driving across from his home near Liverpool.

The B-side was a different story, we recorded the track as before, but Mike wouldn't make the time to come back and add the lead vocal as he said he was busy with gigs, although Sierra were anxious to get the single finished and released.

Sometimes when Steve and I were writing we would get a friend of ours, Mike Stacey (aka Mike Craft) to sing the vocal to make a bit of a change from me doing it. Mike had sung the lead vocal on the demo of 'Brothers and Sisters' which was meant to be the B-side of the Mike Pender single, and if you have the Mike Pender single, you have Mike Stacey/Craft singing the B-side — we used the demo on Mike's record!

Matt and I had some serious conversations about the future, I had been wrong to feel that things might be okay at PRT as they had now dropped me as I had feared, although Matt really wanted my next album to be on Sierra Records, although the budgets wouldn't be the same. My financial situation was looking dire.

By now Pam and I had split, I won't go into details, but we were trying to make a fresh start although the kids had taken it very badly.

I was about to go through a period of burying my head, feeling positive one minute and broken the next, but still trying to function as a musician, keeping my true feelings from everyone around me. I'm good at that, I'm an idiot.

Steve and I were still writing regularly, I had moved the studio and was trying to carry on as close to normal as possible with regular visits from Steve from his home in the Northeast to write and record new material.

By now, I had agreed a new record deal with Matt to put my new album *Rock Solid* on Sierra Records and the writing sessions were going well although I felt I needed help on the production side to get the best performances possible onto tape.

Steve's material was published by DJM, as I mentioned before, but a share was owned by Gus Dudgeon, who had produced one of the Colin Blunstone albums I'd sung on, and Gus had heard some rough mixes of some of our current songs which he really liked.

To cut a long story short, I really wanted some outside input at this stage, told Matt that I wanted to get Gus involved (it was expensive), Matt agreed and sorted it out and soon Gus joined us in the studio.

By now it was 1988, I was in a relationship with Rita who had been a friend initially but now our relationship was closer, and we were living together. Rita had just had a difficult divorce and I guess we were both damaged but leaning on each other trying to make it right.

Gus was quite a character, a real eccentric who was used to the best of everything I guess — Matt was unimpressed when Gus's manager (his wife, affectionately known as 'The Sheriff') demanded a car to take Gus from his home in Cobham, Surrey, To Kings Cross Station, insisting the car must have a phone, and of course first-class travel on the train.

We had a spare, en-suite bedroom at home, so Gus stayed with us, and he had a special routine that surprised, and amused us all.

Every day Gus would awake, roll a huge spliff, get into the bath and smoke it before getting out and dressed into a colour coded outfit for the day.

Every day would be different, but fully colour-matched for example it might be a yellow tracksuit, yellow socks and trainers topped off with yellow-rimmed glasses. I expect his underpants were yellow too but can't guarantee that.

Nicely relaxed, Gus would come down to the studio and promptly turn the speaker volume to deafening and start the day's work.

Gus liked to work loud, and he also had a reputation for working his musicians, especially singers very hard, meaning that when it came to recording vocals on the tracks, he would keep insisting that I "just do another one", over and over and over again until I was exhausted, and my voice was shot.

I didn't get it, to be honest Gus didn't get the best out of me.

A few days after we started our sessions, Gus announced that he needed to break for a week to go to a studio in Amsterdam to prepare for the recording of Elton John's new album.

I asked Gus what 'preparations' he was meant to be doing for a whole week and he said, "getting a drum sound". Good grief!

Steve and I recorded three tracks with Gus over this period at my studio and Sierra records chose two of them, 'Heart to Heart' and 'I Want You' to be released as a single, which Gus wanted to mix at Marquee Studios in London. The third track 'I'm on your side' was included on my *Rock Solid* album released in 1989 on Sierra Records.

I remember sitting in the reception area at the Marquee, listening to the same drum pattern over and over again until they were happy with the sound, which to me sounded just like it did before they started.

Hey-ho, I guess you have to sell some studio time...

Sadly, Gus died in 2002 alongside his wife Sheila ('The Sheriff'), they were found in their car near the M4 motorway where Gus apparently fell asleep at the wheel causing the car to leave the road and crash.

Steve and I attended the funeral, where Elton John spoke fondly of Gus, saying they had been planning to work together again soon when he heard of the tragedy.

R.I.P Gus you were one of a kind.

Gus's influence on my career was not restricted to the recordings we did together. As I have mentioned before Steve Thompson and I were effectively signed to different publishing companies for our joint works, with Steve's fifty per cent administered by Dick James Music whilst my share was with my own publisher, Verity Music.

Unbeknown to Steve and me, DJM had submitted one of our songs for the *Eurovision Song Contest*, 'I Want You', but first to become the UK entry it had to be entered for *A Song for Europe*. Eight songs were nominated for *A Song for Europe*, and 'I Want You' was one of them meaning I was going to have to appear on a BBC TV show, competing against the other seven entries to select the UK entry for *Eurovision*.

Clearly, I couldn't do this, it would ruin what credibility I had as a rock artist in one fell swoop, so we had to find someone else to do it, double quick.

Mike Stacy/Craft was an excellent singer, soon to be elevated to huge success with the Smokie, for the moment he was simply a very good session singer, therefore available — but was he willing?

Yep, Mike was keen to do it, so we substituted him in my place and got down work preparing him for the show.

Our version of 'I Want You' was a really soulful track with great feel so it was very important to make sure we could get this feel onto TV to make the best of our chances, but when the contract came through from the BBC our hopes were dashed.

The rules had changed for this year's show, and all the acts were told they had to use the BBC Orchestra. Disaster!

The contract also said that the UK entry had to be solely about music, not 'image' and any gimmicks or scanty clothing would guarantee disqualification, which wasn't a problem to us as we weren't intending to use anything scanty or gimmicky!

Mike was going to be dressed pretty conservatively, as were our backing vocalists, George Lamb, Phil Caffrey and Elli Luha.

So, we prepared for the night, the presenter, Terry Wogan made the announcement, Mike looked great and sung the song really well, although the orchestra was stiff, and definitely not soulful meaning the audience really didn't get to hear the best of our song.

This wasn't the worst of it though, as the eventual winner of *A song for Europe* was scantily dressed, and used a pre-recorded backing track — what happened to 'the rules?'

I think we came fifth and as only the song in first place was to be the UK entry for *Eurovision* that was the end of it for us, although the UK entry 'Only The Light' performed by Rikki only came thirteenth out of twenty-two competing countries, the worst performing UK entry so far.

This Rock 'n' Roll Won't Last You Know!

19
On The Move Again

Financially things were getting tight again, I was happy to be involved with Matt Haywood, with my stuff on Sierra Records but it was early days for the label, with not a lot of money around to pay artists large advances, it was worrying.

Time for a new plan, we had been looking for a new place to live, not too expensive but still with enough space for a studio when a place came up out in the countryside in the Yorkshire Dales. Many Bradford families would make trips to the Dales to get fresh air and beautiful scenery when I was a kid, and my family was no exception.

As a child I would long to live somewhere like that away from the hustle-bustle, so it seemed only natural to look for something around the Settle area, on the main A65 heading for the Dales and eventually the Lake District.

We found somewhere perfect for us, that had been repossessed and was open to offers, it was called Israel Cottage and it needed some TLC, but we made an offer, and it was accepted. Pretty soon we were heading North to make yet another new start.

Israel Cottage, Eldroth, close to Clapham, North Yorkshire was just right for us, far enough from neighbours to be sure of not disturbing anyone and a small barn attached which was just right for a studio. We contacted Billy Barton again, to do the necessary building work and carpentry, and pretty soon the studio was up and running again.

I had a plan, sure that previous clients would want to come to this beautiful place to make music with me, overlooking Ingleborough, Whernside and Pen-Y-Ghent in the distance — you could see all three peaks from the studio window.

I was sure this would be my home forever...

With the 'Israel' studio up and running I began contacting former clients in the hope that they would want to join me in this beautiful place, but my timing was poor with the music business in the UK going through major changes, meaning many of my previous clients were struggling.

I still had my album *Rock Solid* to finish for Sierra Records but that was unlikely to bring any quick money in, although I would need to finance a new lineup of the band to promote it when it did come out.

Out of the blue I got a call from Ray Minhinnett, which was a bit of a surprise as our last interaction wasn't so great.

A while back Ray had approached me to help him finish some demos to help him to get a record deal which of course I did, and when the demos were finished, I introduced him to Matt, who was still at PRT.

Matt liked what he heard, and I waited for news, expecting to be contacted with a schedule to record an album with Ray but was surprised to find out that he'd gone to another producer. When I approached Ray to say I had thought, as I had helped him to get the deal, I would be producing the album he simply said, "I have to do what's best for me".

Oh well, I suppose it's best to leave stuff like that in the past and move on...

Ray was now playing guitar in John Coghlan's Diesel — John was formerly the drummer in Status Quo but now had his own band and they wanted me to join them for a European tour that was due to start soon.

Bearing in mind my current situation the timing was right, so I accepted the offer, met up with Ray, John and bassist Jeff Brown to finalise the details.

On moving to Israel Cottage, I had begun to check out what was going on locally, to try to connect with my neighbours, which can be quite difficult in rural areas where outsiders aren't always welcome. The nearest town was Settle, about seven miles away down country lanes, but I discovered the nearest pub to home was only a couple of miles away, the Flying Horseshoe, close to the Settle-Carlisle railroad where you could often see steam trains go by.

The regulars at 'The Shoe' were mostly farmers, but I managed to fit in, enough to be able to while away a few hours before driving home along narrow lanes, slightly the worse for wear.

One evening soon after we had moved to 'Israel' I was driving home and seeing a car approaching pulled into a passing place to give way only to see that the car was actually a police car.

I sat nervously as the driver of the car pulled alongside and wound his window down, gesturing for me to do the same.

Seeing that I was nervous the copper said "Are you the new lad from Israel Cottage? been to the 'Shoe, have you? Don't worry the only time we have any problems at night on these roads late at night is when someone drives around sober."

I didn't laugh, until he'd driven away but I couldn't believe my luck, I'd been a bit too heavy with the port and brandies with one of the local farmers who had them as his regular tipple. Rock 'n' Roll!

On another expedition I found High Bentham and discovered a pub/hotel where live music was featured regularly, got chatting to the landlord, a friendly Scot by the name of John, who had a furious taste for alcohol and loved sharing it. John was a real music fan so I told him about the Diesel Band and our need for a place to rehearse, at which point he said we could rehearse there but also the guys could stay there if needed.

The Coach House became the band's base for a while, it was perfect for us.

A couple of rehearsals later we were ready to go, and the band sounded good, playing nice rocky/ soulful material that was right up my street, we were ready to rock!

Germany was the first port of call, but before we got to the ferry the guys had a surprise for me when I was informed that the lineup for this tour had been announced, with Bernie Marsden on guitar!

If anyone asked, I had to be Bernie! I wasn't going to do that, but said nothing at the time, as we grabbed the ferry with our truck full of gear and headed for Germany with our roadie and sound guy Mick at the wheel.

The tour was just what you might expect, sweaty gigs, long journeys, too much partying and huge hangovers — I remember falling down at least one flight of stairs due to wobbly legs after a gig.

We just loved playing, and even set some gear up at a hotel we were staying at on a day off to play some music for the other residents, with one of us (I don't remember who) playing the whole set with his trousers around his ankles.

The atmosphere did begin to sour after a while though as there was rivalry between Ray and Jeff that looked as if it might turn nasty. But it was Jeff and I who nearly came to blows when we wrestled each other to the ground angrily, eventually reaching a stalemate with both of us having a grip on the other and collapsing into peals of laughter.

So, we ended the run of gigs and headed for the ferry, hoping to share the money we'd earned and go home for a break much more well off than when we started.

It didn't work out like that though, too much partying and therefore spending money meant there was precious little share out at the end, meaning I went home with just a few pounds in my pocket.

Soon after we got back, I suggested we get together at "Israel to do some recording, which we did, laying down a couple of really nice tracks, and then we went out to do some UK gigs to try and make some money. It soon became pretty apparent that it wasn't going to work financially though, and the project just fizzled out and we all went our separate ways again.

Good times though.

Back to reality, I had an album to finish. Jeff visited 'Israel' a couple of times whilst I was working, and even contributed to a couple of tracks on the album.

It was easy to get down to work, with no real distractions and pretty soon it was completed, ready to send to Matt, who seemed happy with it, and we were ready to get it out onto the market. For me it meant getting back to finding people for a new band lineup, but first something came up that would delay me for a couple of weeks but bring some much-needed cash in.

Steve Waite got in touch, he had some guys in a band that he was involved with, The Works, who needed to do some recording and wanted to know if they could come to the studio. We fixed a rate and when they arrived, we started to make some progress but one of the guitarists didn't seem to be working out and I don't believe we actually finished anything.

As they left, I gave them a copy of *Rock Solid* and they hit the road, heading for the Northeast where they all lived.

Back to the job in hand, finding a new JV Band to promote *Rock Solid* I was racking my brains when I had a phone call from the band that had just left the studio, saying they'd like to be my new band, and they had learned the songs on *Rock Solid*.

They knew a village hall near where they lived, where we could rehearse if I fancied giving it a try? I felt I had nothing to lose, so we arranged to meet and try things out at Kirby Sigston Village Hall, on the A19 heading towards Teesside, about sixty miles from home.

I loaded some gear into the car and set off wondering what to expect, although I knew the guys were decent enough players I wondered how they would interpret my songs.

On arrival I could see they were already set up and ready to go so I got my stuff organised, asked what they'd like to start with, counted the first song in and wow! They knew the song better than I did, and that was the case for everything we played that day, amazing.

Big smiles all round and I had my new band, Craig Ellis on drums, Brian West on bass, and Terry Swain on guitar and keyboards, all lovely guys and great players, life was good!

I returned home and proceeded to fix up some gigs so we could start promoting the album with this new lineup, hoping I could generate enough money to keep it going. The guys were happy to be patient about that aspect of it until we got things working properly and I really hoped we could make it work.

We had put together a new version of one of mine and Steve Thompson's songs, 'Looking for Love' and it was a real improvement on the original version, so we recorded a new version that sounded really great, I was really hoping for the best with this lineup.

This Rock 'n' Roll Won't Last You Know!

20
Guilt Is A Heavy Load...

Despite the positives with the new band, all was not well at home, and as usual it was down to me, and as usual I was burying my head in the sand, focusing on my music despite problems in my personal life.

I had an agreement with Pam to have the kids for weekends and at first it seemed to be working well. My neighbours at Israel Farm just next door were happy to let the kids see the animals, even watching a sheep give birth one time, and they seemed to be loving the open space of the countryside, but something wasn't right of course.

Their Dad had a new wife, and I was expecting too much of them to just accept this.

I had terrible feelings of guilt at the way I'd abandoned them, and I just didn't know how to deal with it or share these feelings with anyone. I felt such a failure, unable to hold together personal relationships and making the same mistakes over and over again.

I began to spend more time in the pub and mixing with the wrong people while Rita was trying to carry on as normal despite still having to cope with the breakdown of her previous marriage, plus our dire financial position.

It wasn't long before I found myself having to make the trip to Skipton, to our building society to admit that we were having problems meaning we might have to put the house on the market and perhaps even miss some mortgage payments.

I thought it best to be honest, but I wasn't prepared for what would come next.

As I took the main A65 from Skipton to Settle it was hard not to think out the dreams I had had when first moving to Israel Cottage, where everything seemed so perfect.

The location was amazing, overlooking the Three Peaks in the distance, the house itself picture perfect, remote enough to work long into the night in the studio with no fear of disturbing anyone as I worked.

Driving the winding minor roads from Settle to Eldroth I passed landmarks that I had passed a thousand times, and as turned into the long track leading past Israel Farm to the cottage, at the very top of the hill, my heart was truly broken at this failure to make it work.
It had seemed so perfect.

As I turned the last corner, to the garden gate I was jolted back to the current reality of our situation. I was shocked to see that the letterbox on the front door had been taped up, and as I ran to the door and tried to get in I discovered the lock had been changed.

In the time it had taken to get from Skipton to the cottage, the building society had obviously sent a locksmith to do this and shut me out of the property. The bastards.

I knew that one of the upstairs window locks was poor so went to my neighbour, Wilson to borrow a ladder, climbed up and got into the bedroom, down to the front door and opened it. I removed the offending lock and the tape over the letterbox, drove to the hardware store in Settle to buy a new lock and within an hour had the cottage under my control again.

The following day I drove to Skipton again, intending to confront the manager at the building society but realising in my current frame of mind it could turn really nasty decided instead to go the Citizens Advice office for help.

I got lucky that day, as a retired lawyer who was volunteering at the office wrote out the template for my letter to the building society, demanding time to get the cottage on the market and remove my possessions in an orderly manner, giving Rita and myself time to sort ourselves out properly.

It worked, and with a heavy heart I set about planning my next move...

21
The Tricky Truck

Rita was making her own plans, and I had decided that the best thing I could do under the circumstances was to get the studio out of there as quickly as possible.

With nowhere to go yet, I made the decision to put the equipment into a truck — a mobile studio. Searching the advertisements in *Exchange and Mart* I found the ideal vehicle, a 'Mini Artic' which was an articulated truck just under the size and weight of a full-size truck, therefore legal to drive on a normal license.

The tractor unit was a Bedford CF, and the trailer big enough to make into a mobile studio, with somewhere for me to sleep until I got myself sorted.

As a result of the Diesel Band gigs and rehearsals at the Coach House in High Bentham I had made friends who I would meet for drinks at other pubs in the area. One of these pubs was The Masons, in Ingleton where I had become friendly with the Landlord Kevin Murphy and his wife Carol who I approached for help as I needed somewhere to park the truck while I worked on it.

The Masons had a huge car park, and they were happy to let me park the truck there, so I parked it out of the way, alongside a factory building belonging to a local engineering firm, who kindly allowed me to run power from a socket in the factory so that I could begin work on converting the truck to a studio.

The next few months were spent working on my latest 'studio'.

I lined the internal walls of the trailer, finishing it off with carpet on the floor and walls, and cut holes to fit windows — the type you see in caravans so that I had some daylight in there.

The front of the trailer was 'Luton' style, with a raised area perfect for resting the mixing desk and speakers on, and I created a pod above with rows of 19" sections to house the rack-mount effects units. The trailer had a pull-down shutter at the rear, so I built a wall just inside, with a caravan door in it so that when I was working in the studio, I could leave the shutter up and enter/leave easily through the door.

Once all the construction work was finished, I bought a bed settee so that I could sleep comfortably in the trailer. For a while my daily routine would begin with the short walk to The Masons, where I would do the cleaning before walking back to the truck to continue the wiring and testing of the equipment. Back to a new reality...

Pretty soon my new studio was up and running, sounding just fine although once completed I had to gingerly climb into the driver's seat of the CF to see if the tractor unit would actually pull the trailer now that all the studio gear was in there! Thankfully it did, slowly but surely.

Meanwhile money was getting tight, so I agreed to take on more duties at The Masons, working as the cook in the small kitchen making what was typical pub food at the time. I had never eaten a fried egg in my life and here I was cooking them!

Oh well, needs must and to be honest it kept me busy enough to forget my troubles for a while, and leisure time was often spent in The Masons with my pal Neil Gowland playing pool and drinking too much.

By now, my new mobile studio had acquired the nickname the 'Tricky Truck', and although I was happy with its current location in The Masons carpark, several moves would be necessary over the next couple of years.

By this time I had begun a relationship with Melinda, and we decided to live together. Melinda had two children with her former partner Andy and had moved to an apartment in nearby Burton in Lonsdale with the girls, Kaley and Jessica.

I realise now that this was far too early to commit to a new relationship, especially with children involved but here I was, making yet another mistake, true to form. The relationship didn't last long, predictably, and another move was soon on the cards.

When I moved in with Melinda, I moved the Tricky Truck to the car park behind the flats where we lived. Luckily, I had begun to get some session work again which was bringing in some much-needed money, meaning I was making regular trips to London on the train from Lancaster.

Chris White, as always was incredibly generous putting work my way whenever possible and this was a real lifeline at the time — Chris you're a Gentleman, and a great friend in need.

The writing, however, was on the wall and my time in Burton in Lonsdale was soon to end but not before a project that came out of the blue to record a bunch of Led Zeppelin tracks.

One of the things I have to do on behalf of my publishing company, Verity Music is to make sure I register all my songs on the PRS/MCPS database, and I received a letter one day enquiring why I had neglected to register some songs just released on an album.

I didn't recognise the songs in question and contacted PRS to find out more, to be told that they were on a compilation album *The British German Connection,* released through a label called Tring International.

I contacted Tring International, and they insisted they had obtained the tracks legitimately but were reluctant to tell from where, although they were prepared to pay me for my 'inconvenience' and wanted to offer me another project as a sweetener.

Tring were thinking of putting out a series of albums called *Bootleg* and wanted me to do *Bootleg Zeppelin.* I was really interested in trying to recreate the Zeppelin stuff, so we agreed a deal and I contacted the current drummer and bassist of my band to do it.

John Clark (drums) and Dave Kinley (bass) had been playing with me for a while as I tried to get back on my feet again, and we were just doing gigs around the Lancaster/ Kendal areas to get established.

I booked the Village Hall in Burton in Lonsdale for a day/night and drove the Tricky Truck down there to record the tracks. Technically it was pretty simple, John and Dave would be in the village hall with headphones on so they could hear what was going on, including my guitar and guide vocal — I was outside in the truck, engineering, playing, and singing.

I ran mic lines from the truck to the hall for the drums, and for a direct input for Dave's bass, with my little Fender Champ in the truck with me for my guide guitar parts.

As it was wintertime, we had an electric fire to try to heat the hall — more on this later!

John and Dave had swotted up on the songs we were about to play, and I had bought a book of Led Zeppelin music that I would use to get the chords and words right as we worked through each track.

John and Dave were just brilliant that day and we laid down the basic tracks for fourteen songs in one session, as requested by Tring International for the planned CD release.

At one point as we were playing Dave and John stopped suddenly and shouted for me to come in quickly, there was an emergency! I ran into the hall to see that the mains cable connected to the electric fire had melted through and you could see the red-hot metal cores of the wire! I quickly disconnected it, and we continued working, in the cold, to complete the tracks.

Once we had all the tracks down, I arranged to keep the hall for a few hours the next day to add the recorder parts for 'Stairway To Heaven'.

I had contacted a local school and recruited Emma Smith, Rachel Hipple, Angela Aldridge and Doug Drake to play the parts and they did the job admirably.

Finally, my good friend Neil Gowland, a brilliant guitarist recorded the 12-string guitar parts on 'Stairway To Heaven', making the basic tracks complete. Job done!

In recent days my relationship with Melinda had broken down completely — this time I have to say it was not all my fault, so the next move for the Tricky Truck was back to The Masons car park, where I completed and mixed the album, and sent the results to Tring International.

With the album ready to be released, the label asked me if I'd be interested in going on the road to promote it, and of course I said yes, I would be up for it if we could do it properly.

I knew that John and Dave would love to do it, as Zeppelin stuff is challenging, but really nice to play, and of course it meant there would be a bunch of well-paid gigs to do.

Unfortunately, my next conversation with Tring would put paid to the gigging side of the project, when they asked to get someone in the band who looked like Robert Plant!

The guy I was dealing with said "you look like Jimmy Page, but we need someone who looks like Robert Plant in the band". When I said that I'd be singing all the lead vocals he suggested we *"get a Robert Plant lookalike to play tambourine or something"!!*

I guess we would have been the first 'tribute band', not my scene at all.

On the day that the situation with Melinda came to a head I had a huge row with her father, who was somewhat of an important figure locally having been a successful businessman for a number of years. It appears he was also a Freemason, which spelled trouble for me.

A while after the split I had a telephone call from the police in Settle, asking me to call in and see them sometime. I was curious so made my way to the police station only to find that I was in trouble, or more to the point I was being accused of threatening to kill someone.

The police said they had a recording of me threatening to kill Melinda, but when I demanded to hear it, they said it wasn't available. Strange!

I'm guessing that Melinda's father's funny handshake cronies were allegedly behind this, although I have no proof of course. Anyway, pretty soon I was called to appear at the Magistrates Court in Ingleton, the accusation having been made official, and to be honest I was really worried as it felt like a small-town issue that could go badly wrong for me.

I was worried unnecessarily, as the Magistrates saw through it right away and I was released without charge, a waste of everyone's time.

After this trauma, things went pretty well for a while, and I was gigging regularly although there were a number of changes in the band lineup as time went by. Luckily, I was usually able to attract good players and the band was building a nice reputation.

The first time John Clark wasn't available for a gig he said he knew someone who would be really good to fill in for him, and he said he'd pass on a tape of my set for the guy to learn and give him details of the venue.

I arrived at the gig on the day and could hear someone practicing drums behind a screen by the stage, so I called out to get his attention, and was shocked to see this young kid appear, clutching a pair of drumsticks!

Cripes! John had sent a child to play for me, was my first feeling but I calmed down and politely introduced myself to John Powney.

I watched as John sat at his drum set, not really knowing what to expect, although of course I trusted John Clark's judgement it was still a bit of a shock to encounter someone so young in a serious gigging situation.

I need not have been concerned, because the second we struck up to run through the first song John's drumming was fantastic. What a player!

Of course there will be those reading this who are familiar with John Powney's work over the years with major bands and in education, he's simply brilliant, and I'm glad we got to work together in his formative years.

Other notable JV Band drummers in this period include Mark Langdon and Vic Edwards.

When Dave Kinley wasn't available, I liked to use Gary Thistlethwaite, and for a brief time Simon Willan filled the bass shoes. Neil Gowland joined us for a while on guitar too when we were a four piece.

Things were actually looking good, the Tricky Truck was relocated to yet another pub car park at The Goat Gap Inn some time later when I moved into a small apartment on a farm just across the A65 from the pub, although it felt like time for a change if I was going anywhere with my career.

The new lady in my life, Karen was a fitness instructor, self employed so with no real ties in that sense although of course her family was in the area.

There were so many bad feelings and unpleasant memories in this part of the world, and I just wanted to get off! My gut feeling was to head south again with the Tricky Truck to make a fresh start away from all the aggravation of recent years, and maybe just travel back to do gigs occasionally with the best of the musicians I'd found here in the Lancaster/Kendal areas.

It sounded like a plan, so I put it to Karen, and she said she'd come with me.

The next few months were spent searching for somewhere to live within striking distance of my friends and contacts in the south, maybe not in the St Albans area as it was too expensive but a little further out — Bedfordshire seemed like a good bet.

In the end we discovered the village of Ickwell, close to Sandy and Biggleswade on the A1 which seemed like a good bet as it was convenient to strike north or south for gigs.

We found the place in Ickwell through an estate agent although the owner of the property was literally next door, in the most striking house in the village.

The village is dominated by the village green, leading most people to refer to the place as Ickwell Green, with its Cricket Club a major part of village activities as is often the case in places like this.

We signed the contract, paid the deposit, and set off back to pack up and leave town.

We didn't need a removal van as we had the Tricky Truck, so everything went on board the trailer with the studio, we said our farewells and hit the road with Karen driving her car behind.

Fully loaded the Tricky Truck was slow, and we had opted to go the M6-M1 route that day which meant a hazardous twenty-mile drive along winding roads to reach the M6, and of course it didn't go smoothly.

About ten miles into our journey I was making a steep left-hand turn, slowly and carefully when an impatient driver cut me up making me hit the kerb with one of the four nearside trailer wheels. I was angry but didn't think too much of it and carried on driving until oncoming traffic began furiously flashing me, so I looked for somewhere to pull over my forty-foot-long vehicle to check for damage.

As I jumped out of the cab, I immediately saw the problem, there were flames gushing from one of the rear wheels with thick black smoke licking up the side of the trailer. Luckily, I had a fire extinguisher in the trailer, and put out the fire.

Two of the good friends I had sadly left behind in Ingleton, Alan and Antoinette ran a garage there and Alan restored classic cars — he was a genius! I called them for advice, and Alan said simply remove the offending wheel and continue carefully on three wheels at the rear, it would be safe if I took my time, and a proper repair would take time as the axle was probably bent.

I had no choice really, and taking my time was the only option as the poor old CF was struggling to pull the fully loaded trailer anyway, so I hit the road again, heading for the M6 and our new home.

Driving south on the M6 past Lancaster there is quite a steep incline, I hadn't really noticed it before but on this journey, it was really obvious, and I couldn't get any more than twenty miles an hour out of the Tricky Truck, making me ever so popular with other traffic heading south.

We pulled into the next services, and I suggested that Karen went ahead in the car, and I'd see her later, much later...

It was a very stressful journey, and you can imagine I was very glad, many hours later to reach Ickwell Green, and my bed.

The place we had rented included access to a garage right next to the house, and the driveway leading to the garage was long enough to fit the Tricky Truck, so before my day was finished, I had to manoeuvre into the driveway safely, lock up and, finally, breathe a huge sigh of relief.

Although we had found the place through an estate agent in nearby Shefford it turned out that the owner's son, Michael Adams was our contact, he appeared to be managing the property and was also living in one of the apartments in the building.

Michael seemed quite friendly, and it seemed handy to have easy access to the person managing the property in case of any problems.

It was January 1993, time for a fresh start and we soon settled into our new life in Ickwell, beginning to look for gigs in the area, now close enough to old friends and colleagues to put a new band together here.

Although Bob and Jim were still technically with The Kinks, they were touring less, meaning there were opportunities for us to work together again — a southern lineup of the JV Band was on the cards, and I could travel north to work with a northern lineup for gigs there.

Work started to come in for the Tricky Truck, and once again my old friend Chris White would travel up from his home in London to record with me.

As work started to pick up for the band, we bought a small box trailer to carry the equipment, pulled by Karen's very nice Ford Escort with its powerful diesel engine.

Things were falling into place; we were making friends locally and the move that had seemed so risky was working out for us. We were doing gigs with the two lineups as planned, I was working with clients in the truck and had begun to record ideas for my own new CD, putting down song ideas and planning to release something soon, life was good, and we were happy with our lot.

In the late summer of 1993 We set off for one of those northern trips, with a run of shows including a well-attended outdoor gig in Kendal Market Square.

It was a beautiful day as we headed south on the M6 after the Kendal show, intending to stop off for a final gig at The Longlands Hotel, a regular haunt where bands would play a Monday night slot to a full house, so we were looking forward to ending this run of dates there.

Our conversation was interrupted when my phone rang, and Karen answered it. Pretty soon it was obvious that there was something wrong and she passed the phone to me.

It was the police, someone had broken into my truck, and "it looks like everything has gone," said the officer.

Shocked, I told him we were about four and a half hours away and we'd get there as soon as possible.

I passed the phone to Karen and asked her to call and cancel the gig at the Longlands, apologising, although I knew they would understand.

She then rang John Clark and asked him to tell the others.

The drive back was horrendous.

There was stuff in that truck that I had cherished for years, vintage microphones and rare pieces of kit that I'd managed to hang on to despite all my recent struggles, what was I going to do to get through this one.

Karen reminded me that we had insured the contents of the truck through our bank, but this was little consolation to me, as a lot of the gear would be hard to replace.

Some of the rackmount units were quite rare now, as were the microphones I had collected.

The journey home seemed to take forever, and as we pulled up outside, I couldn't wait to get into the truck to see what had happened.

As I stepped through the door of the Tricky Truck the truth was there in front of me — the policeman was right, nearly everything was gone, it was as if someone had fitted out a recording studio, and it was now time to install the equipment.

The multitrack tape machines were gone, the mixing desk was gone, the overhead racks were empty, and even the wiring was gone. The microphones were gone, a guitar, keyboards, amplifiers, speakers the lot, the only things left were the large JBL monitors — probably because they were too big to get through the door, as I'd built the rear wall after loading the JBL's into the truck.

I was devastated, all the crap I'd been through in previous years came back to me, the only things I'd manage to keep throughout these times had been in the truck and I felt like I'd lost everything after all.

We went into the house, as the police had questions.

I didn't feel they were particularly sympathetic at first, in fact it seemed to me that they thought this was an 'inside job'. I may be wrong but that is how it felt.

I was empty, I just couldn't believe this had happened just when things seemed to be working out for us, and I really didn't see a way out of this situation until Karen reminded me that of course we still had the gigging equipment that was with us on our trip to Kendal.

We approached the insurance company to make a claim so that I could try to re-equip the studio somehow, but they responded to tell us they weren't prepared to cover the majority of the equipment. I was shocked and contacted the bank to try to clear this up as the bank had arranged the cover in the first place.

At our meeting, the bank manager was also shocked to hear that my claim had been rejected as he was sure that the policy, he had arranged would cover everything fully.

As proof of this he made a call to the insurance section while I was sitting there, asking for a quote for a customer needing cover for exactly the same equipment/location that I had claimed for, and a policy was approved!

He then told them of my plight, and they said they would look into it, so I left the bank and waited for their response.

When we had first moved to Ickwell I had parked the trailer on the drive belonging to our property, in front of a garage that we had access to, but a short while later our next-door neighbour offered to let me park the trailer on their drive, parallel to its original parking place. I accepted the offer as it meant that we could then have easy access to the garage.

That was my big mistake when it came to my insurance claim, the company were insisting that the trailer was no longer located on my property and therefore not covered by the policy. They would no longer cover any of the items for business use, however as a gesture of goodwill they would cover any items that could be classed as 'domestic' stored in the trailer.

Basically that meant that there were certain items covered, for example an amplifier that I used to power the headphones was a 'domestic' hi-fi amp, a pair of Yamaha NS10 speakers that I had could be classed as 'domestic' and so on. In the end a small amount of stuff was covered but none of the major items like the multi-track tape machines, mixer, outboard equipment, and microphones were not.

The Tricky Truck would be no more, but I did approach the Musicians Union for advice on insuring my instruments and equipment properly in future, and to this day it is covered, by a company specialising in musical instrument cover.

22
Here We Go Again...

The meagre amount that the insurance company paid out allowed me to buy a small amount of recording equipment so that I could record my own stuff in the apartment, although there was no way I could put together a viable recording business facility with it.

On the plus side I had just begun writing equipment reviews for one of the major publications, *Sound On Sound* so I did have access to some amazing deals on the gear I was reviewing.

Mentally I was in a bad place, although determined to find out who was responsible for the theft of my gear.

As well as doing band gigs I was having to do solo shows at smaller venues to make ends meet, and it was at one of these gigs that I had a breakthrough.

I just finished playing a gig at The Bell in Sandy, a when a guy approached me at the bar to complement me on my playing that night.

"Have you ever done any recording" he said, and a little warning light in my head made me respond "no, why?".

"Oh, 'cos I know where there's some hooky recording gear if you're interested."

Of course, I said I was really interested — who had the gear?

"Do you know 'Foxy'", was his reply so I said no and asked if he knew Foxy's address, surprised when he told me straight away the address nearby in Sandy.

I thanked him, packed my gear, and went home, calling my police contact first thing the next morning with the address of the place where I was sure they would find some of my stuff.

The police response was pretty disappointing to be honest, when they told me they'd need a warrant and with the weekend coming up that was unlikely to be possible.

I hung up the phone, jumped into the car and drove to the address

I had been given, stopping off on the way for a six pack of 'Dutch courage', determined to get to the bottom of it myself.

As I pulled up opposite the address I had been given, it was easy to spot where I needed to be going as there was a sign 'Foxie's Lair' next to the door, so I sat there contemplating my next move. I could see that there were people in the house, and that someone was looking across at me so I decided to make a move before they could, running across to the front door just as it was opening.

I burst into the room and could immediately see some of the things from my studio piled against the far wall, and at that point things turned really nasty.

The upshot of it was that I made Foxy tell me where he got the stuff from, and his answer shocked me as he blurted out the name of a close acquaintance.

So was this acquaintance behind all this? A person that I trusted, my neighbour and the person 'keeping an eye' on my studio whilst I was away.

Just then the police arrived and took away my stuff as evidence, gave me a warning not to take things into my own hands and promised to get to the bottom of it, so I went home to cool down, expecting to hear again from the police the next morning.

More disappointment the next day though, to find out that Foxy's father had contacted the police to inform them that it was in fact he who had given the stuff to his son, having bought it at a car boot sale, meaning the police could take it no further. Pathetic.

At least I could now be pretty sure of who was behind the theft, although I still hadn't found the bulk of my equipment, as the equipment recovered from Foxy's was just the headphone amp, the NS10 speakers, a keyboard and a couple of other bits and pieces.

I still have those Yamaha NS10 speakers today, although the fingerprint powder has long since worn off.

The next thing to turn up was a guitar, when the owner of a music shop in Biggleswade called me to say he thought he had one of my guitars, that he'd taken in place of money owed to him. I drove to Biggleswade and sure enough it was my guitar although the guy begged me not to take it further, he was happy to let me have the guitar back but was clearly afraid of the consequences if I went to the police. I didn't take it further.

I was obsessed with finding my stuff and must have been very hard to live with in this period as I was on the case pretty much 24/7.

I remembered that Michael Adams had mentioned a property he had vacant in a nearby village and wondered if perhaps some of my equipment might be there, so I mentioned it to the police who on checking it out discovered cars in the garage that were clearly being 'ringed'. They didn't find anything of mine but clearly there was something illegal going which I believe led to a prison sentence for Michael Adams.

Nothing else turned up despite my enquiries, so I tried to leave this behind and get on with my life although this whole experience had left a mark on me that was about to surface and seriously affect things moving forward.

I just didn't feel right, but I was determined to get back on my feet again, although I had to accept that my days running a commercial studio were over, and I had to get out of this house!

I discovered that there was a relatively new A Level qualification, the A Level in Music Technology, and figured that very few music teachers would have the knowledge to teach this properly. A large part of the qualification involved making music using recently developed music software, an area that I had already investigated as a way to continue my own songwriting/recording activities without the professional equipment that had been stolen from my truck.

One of the companies that I had recently been involved with when demonstrating guitars and amps was also promoting one of the leading music software packages, *Cubase*, so I approached them to see if I could get anything for free.

Success! I was provided with free packages on the proviso that I would provide them with feedback to help with the development of the software, a great result.

As far as computers were concerned, I decided to go with a Windows PC for my project, mainly because it was possible to build your own PC whereas part to build a Mac type computer were not available, meaning that would be the most expensive option.

Pretty soon I had a decent computer music setup ready to go, and now needed some work, and a way to deliver it, but first of all we wanted to get out of the apartment, although we were happy in Ickwell.

We found a solution when a house became available at the other side of the village that would give us a fresh start, and eventually gave us the option to buy, so we went for it despite cracks in our relationship, probably due to my state of mind at the time.

Out of the blue came an invite to perform at a celebration to mark the 40th anniversary of the Fender Stratocaster, alongside other 'Strat' players and guests including Sonny Curtis from The Crickets, Rory Gallagher, Frankie Miller, and Sherman Robertson although I believe that both Hank Marvin and Eric Clapton pulled out at the last minute due to the fact that the whole event was being filmed without their permission.

The show was at the Free Trade Hall in Manchester, and we all travelled up there in coaches provided by the promoter. After the show I had a nice chat in the bar with Rory Gallagher, who remembered me from when I had opened for him years earlier.

Rory was a lovely guy and a great guitar player, such a sad loss when he died far too early a couple of years later, in June 1995 at the age of 47.

I returned home wondering what might be next for Karen and I when just in time, something came up to keep us both busy for a while when Chris White got in touch to tell us he had been working with an amazing young singer, Bianca Kinane, who was involved with producer Pete Waterman and had a new album ready for release.

The record company wanted Bianca to tour to support the album and Chris wanted me to help him put a band together for her, and possibly tour manage the project as well as playing guitar.

This was a bit different, but I accepted the challenge and started to look for the right people, eventually settling on Don Airey on keyboards, Alex Meadows on bass, Carlos Hercules on drums, with Debbie Scamp and Maria Quintele on backing vocals.

I booked the nearby Cricket Club to rehearse the band initially whilst Karen ran through the backing vocals with the girls in our house, until we were all ready to get together and work on the overall performance. It was sounding good.

Chris came up to listen and agreed we'd got it right and we awaited the next move.

The news was good when it came, we were to do a 32-date tour with Jools Holland on the 'Sex, Jazz and Rock 'n' Roll Tour', which was a perfect opportunity for Bianca to establish herself properly.

Bianca had first her first break on the TV show *Stars In Their Eyes* when she appeared as Maria Carey — all the acts on the show had to appear in the guise of a famous artist and were judged on how close they could get their performance to the original.

At the age of 16 Bianca won the show, and although it was an amazing break she had struggled to establish herself as a valid artist since, and this was now her chance.

Jools is a lovely guy, very generous and there were none of the silly games I'd experienced when opening in the past from anyone in the crew, there was a great atmosphere from start to finish on this tour.

By the time I had hired all the musicians, booked hotels, and hired two vehicles to get us around, the budget I had been given was proving to be really tight.

There was no money left to hire crew, I would have to drive one of the vehicles and one of the band would need to drive the other, and no one wanted to do it, causing an atmosphere between us before we even started.

In the end Carlos agreed to drive one vehicle with the rest of the guys, and I would drive the other, with Bianca and the girls, and we were ready to hit the road for a major tour across the UK. By and large the gigs were excellent, despite a strained atmosphere with the male contingent at times, more of which I'm not going to get into here, because it's not worth the time.

Bianca sang like an angel — she's still my favourite female vocalist, after all these years and has featured on several of my own albums, and the band turned in a creditable performance each night.

The highlight of the tour was probably the Royal Albert Hall where we played to a full house and Bianca really impressed, despite a setback in the afternoon when the venue jobsworths were being absolute ratbags. Our routine at each show would usually involve the band sound checking whilst the girls went around the venue putting Bianca's flyers on the seats, next to Jools flyers.

Nothing unusual about that except at the Royal Albert Hall, shortly after we'd returned to our dressing room after soundcheck, there was a loud knock on the door and a member of staff entered demanding a large amount of money in payment for putting our flyers on the seats.

An argument between him and me had just started when Jools's tour manager, passing our dressing room at the right moment, overheard the row and told me they had just made the same demand for Jools's flyers. He told the guy to stop hassling us, and that there would be no payment from either band, reassuring me that there would be no comeback from this, the guy was just being a twat.

Okay, so we got on with the show, and the rest of the tour until all the dates were completed and we headed for home again, keen to see if the tour would have any impact on Bianca's career.

Despite the hard work and Bianca's brilliant performances the record company decided, for their own reasons not to get behind the album, and it was back to square one for Bianca.

There really is no fairness in this industry and I guess I'm a fool to expect it, but I have always tried to think positively in my music career despite the disappointments and really hoped this one would work out for Bianca.

On a personal level, things were really no better between Karen and me when we got back home, we struggled on for a while, but Karen and I were growing apart, to be honest I felt that she was falling out of love with me, and maybe some time apart might help us both to work things out.

'Being apart' meant me moving out, and I found a tiny cottage for rent in the next village, Northill, just a little too close the local pub, the Kings Arms which I was already familiar with as it was the closest pub to Ickwell and the haunt of many Ickwell locals.

Just before I made the move I had been diagnosed with clinical depression and had begun a course of treatment — Prozac.

One evening in the Kings Arms I was offered a drink by one of the locals who had spotted that something was wrong. I accepted and pretty soon we were telling each other our problems and it turned out he was on leave from work suffering from depression, taking Prozac too.

I wish I could tell you it was the start of a beautiful friendship, but I can't, we were really bad for each other, beginning a routine involving drinking at the pub from opening time until closing time each day until we were no use to man nor beast.

Luckily, I soon realised it had to stop although in the meantime my doctor had changed my medication to Seroxat, as the Prozac didn't seem to be working.

The effects of Seroxat are probably what made me pull myself together.

Alone in the cottage I had begun to have suicidal thoughts, I'm sure down to the effects of Seroxat, although I was able to keep myself together enough to do a job I had managed to secure, lecturing for two days a week at Luton Sixth Form College, teaching Music Technology.

I had to do something about this situation and teaching might be a way out of this mess, so determined to make a go of it I approached my friends Lin and Elaine Eversden for help.

I had been looking into the possibility of getting a small, manoeuvrable vehicle to build a portable teaching vehicle to take to schools that might hire me, complete with equipment they didn't have, and had discovered that ambulances were 'pensioned off' after a certain amount of service and you could buy them direct from the Ambulance Service.

An ambulance might be the perfect vehicle and I knew that Lin would be the perfect guy to help me fit it out, so I put myself on the waiting list for a vehicle.

By now the Tricky Truck was parked in the Kings Arms carpark, with power running to it, so we could use this as a base for our activities, once we got our ambulance, so we waited for news.

At last! I got the call to collect my ambulance, and Lin and I soon got to work converting it to a teaching unit complete with computers, a small mixer, and speakers.

In no time I was ready to go, and I searched to find out any local schools offering music technology. Pretty soon I had work, with an afternoon at Kingsbrook School in Milton Keynes, an afternoon at Sandy Upper School, and a morning at Bedford School, combined of course with the two days at Luton 6th Form College.

I would simply drive the ambulance to the schools. Plug into the power, and wait for my pupils, perfect. It was looking good, but I still had to sort my health out as I was having bad days too often, although always managing to cover it up when working.

When I wasn't actually working, I was a mess and I had to find a drug-free way of beating this.

Don't ask me what made me do it, but first of all I borrowed a bike and then when that one fell to pieces I went out and bought a good one. I went out every day in between jobs and just cycled for miles and miles, finding it really therapeutic, and feeling definite improvements, finally ceasing to take the Seroxat, and the alcohol.

The resulting come down was pretty extreme, but I stuck with it, sleeping on top of a duvet which would be soaked each morning, hanging it out to dry and repeating the next day.

I can't remember how long it took but it worked, and eventually Karen and I decided to try again, I gave up the cottage in Northill and

I moved back into the house in Ickwell.

I always got the feeling that folks in Ickwell were enjoying the trials that Karen and I were going through, and that sort of coloured my relationship with the village.

Still, I was glad to be giving it another try, and the work/financial situation was looking better, with my teaching work, gigs with the band and Karen's exercise classes all helping to get us by.

I had decided to get a teaching qualification and enrolled on a course at Bedford College with this in mind, soon enjoying the evening classes with like minded people trying to better themselves — although I did think a lot of what we were being taught was irrelevant tosh.

A fellow student Adrian Smith was a technician in the Sound Engineering department at Bedford College, and one night he told me there was a vacancy at the college for a music lecturer. I decided to go for it, was given an interview, actually two interviews and waited for the result. The result was that I got the jobs.

Why two interviews? Well the job involved working for two separate departments at the college, the Engineering Department, which ran the City and Guilds Sound Engineering course, and the Performing Arts Department which ran the BTEC Music and Music Technology courses. I would have two bosses and divide my time between them.

My first task though was to give notice to my current jobs with the ambulance, and that went smoothly enough although the Luton Sixth Form Principal was saddened to get my resignation and offered me more hours, although not enough to tempt me.

I was in at the deep end at Bedford College but soon it was the summer break, giving me time to organise things the way I wanted to do them. Lecturers in Further Education don't get the summer break like schoolteachers do, as the summer is the time to plan for next year.

I completely reorganised the programme for the next academic year, going out on a limb to deliver each programme in a way that I thought would work much better than before. It was risky but I was sure I was right.

September came and the proof was going to be in pudding so to say, and I put my plan into action, although to an extent my plan had been in action all summer. During the summer break I had been running workshops, where students hoping to get the courses would spend a day with me working on the sort of projects they would be doing if they joined us.

Some of it was quite tough, with the result that some prospective entrants would drop out, deciding not to start the course. The result was that from day one in September everyone I had on board was likely to succeed and last the course to the end.

Around this time, I also started accepting work as an examiner.

Most schools and colleges were happy for teaching staff to undertake a certain amount of examining work as it brought with it a little kudos for the main employer.

A Level papers would arrive in packages at home, and I would sit for hours in the ambulance listening, checking, and grading work, and awarding an accurate grade for each piece.

In order to be an examiner, training sessions had to be undertaken, where each candidate would go through a day's standardisation followed by tests to see if they could grade learner work accurately. Those selected would then be sent an amount of work to mark dependant on their performance at the event.

I guess at these sessions you were also watched and assessed for any more senior posts in the organisation because I was soon invited to be a 'Team Leader'. All this was good for the CV, and also had benefits financially.

At Bedford College we were on performance related pay — PRP, with a set of objectives that would determine your pay award each year.

As a result of my plan my course achieved 100% achievement and 100% retention meaning I got an Advanced PRP award for the first time in the college's history.

In my time at Bedford College I rose from a simple Lecturer to Head of Department, although in the end I was finding that I was in college seven days a week to do the job properly, with little energy left for my music, so it couldn't go on...

Things at home weren't great, we had grown apart although still friends, sleeping in separate rooms, being polite and trying our best with neither of us making a decision to change things.

Then one day I got an email saying, "Remember me, it's Carole from Harlow?"

I had often wondered what had happened to Carole, we first met many years earlier when she worked in the music business for the music papers *Sounds*, and *Record Mirror*.

I replied to say of course I remembered her, to be told that she was now living in Scotland.

Although she was living in Scotland, Carole's job meant she had to travel to various parts of the country and as she was due to be in London soon, we arranged to meet at her hotel when she next came down for a meeting.

When the day came, I nervously approached the hotel, wondering how I would feel on meeting someone again who I had not seen for over twenty years, would we still feel a connection, is that possible?

We met for a drink, and sure enough the connection was there, and we got on as if no time had passed, promising to meet again the next time she was in town.

I headed for home feeling good for the first time in ages, so happy that Carole's teenage daughter Hannah had instigated the email that led to our meeting that day and looking forward to meeting Hannah when Carole was next in London.

Although I hadn't said anything to Karen, I had been feeling there might be someone in the background who was becoming important to her. It was just a feeling, but I hadn't wanted to bring it up.

Recently, she had made a new group of friends and we didn't really socialise as a couple anymore.

The upshot of this was that almost at the same time as I began seeing Carole, I think Karen began seeing Chris and the relationships appear to have developed almost in tandem, although I still wasn't sure about committing to a major change just yet.

At my next meeting with Carole in London, she brought her daughter Hannah who was due to meet her Dad later that day. We met in the hotel where they were staying, and then Hannah's Dad Colin joined us to collect her.

Carole and Colin had parted some time earlier, and they were both now with new partners although in regular contact of course so that Hannah could have regular contact with her Dad.

Over time, Carole and I talked about the possibility of getting together again but in the end, I told her I couldn't bear the idea of yet another marriage failure, and that I was determined to somehow make my relationship with Karen work.

We parted that day saying goodbye again, and I headed for home to try and make my marriage work.

Over the next few days I had this nagging feeling that Karen and I had just become friends sharing a home together, and that what I had said at my last meeting with Carole was really not going to work. Marriage is a partnership and both partners have to be willing to make it work. I called Carole and said I'd like to meet next time she was in London as I had something to tell her, and she agreed, telling me that she had something to tell me too.

The day came, and Carole travelled down from Scotland to Luton Airport to meet me at her hotel.

We chatted for a while, then one of us said "who goes first" so I said I would and explained that I had been thinking about what I had said at our last meeting and come to realise that I was wrong, and that I wanted us to be together if she was okay with that.

Carole responded with bombshell that she had thought it was over between us, had agreed to marry her partner Paul, and that they had, in fact got married a couple of days earlier! Oops!

After the initial shock, we laughed about the situation – you couldn't make it up, could you? and after talking for a while Carole said she had always wanted to be with me and would tell Paul as soon as she got home.

I met Paul some time later, when I attended Hannah's school concert in Scotland, and I apologised for the way things had happened, but Paul was very relaxed about it, simply saying, "It's okay, I knew it would happen".

Twenty years later as I write this, Carole and I are happy together, Chris and Karen are happy together and we're all good friends, so thankfully the right decisions were made twenty years ago — Oh and Paul lives in the Australian Outback with another lady in a house he built himself.

This Rock 'n' Roll Won't Last You Know!

23
A Fresh Start

The year 2003 began with our move together to a house in Cardington Bedfordshire, a beautiful 300-year-old cottage that was once two tiny two-room dwellings although it has now been extended a little to include a kitchen and bathroom.

Although extremely basic, the cottage is perfect for us as it is situated nicely and is detached with no neighbours close enough to hear me making a racket — yes you guessed it, I have a studio here, just right for writing and recording my own stuff and collaborating with others if I wish.

Hannah finished her schooling in Scotland, staying with Carole's mum Barbara who was still living there although the plan was to move them both here as soon as Hannah left school.

We were on the lookout for a place nearby for Barbara and eventually she moved to an Alms house just around the corner from us in Cardington where she lived happily until her death in 2022 at the age of 95.

Hannah was with us until leaving to attend University in London after which she travelled, eventually settling in Australia for a while until she moved to France permanently with her partner Marie.

When Carole and I moved to Cardington I was still at Bedford College and examining for Pearson although I had moved from A Level to the more hands-on, work-related BTEC Qualifications, although my time at the college was soon to come to an end.

I had always had my doubts about the value of A Levels in music and the performing arts, preferring BTEC qualifications where I could properly share my skills and experience in the industry, and through my work with Pearson I could also influence the way that BTEC Qualifications were structured.

When I was offered a senior post with the Pearson organisation, training examiners, and inspecting Colleges I decided to leave Bedford College to pursue this new opportunity, free up some time to get back in the studio at home and focus more on my music career again.

The work for Pearson was mostly done at home meaning I could plan my own time and get back to my first love, making a racket with my guitar.

I was able to spend enough time in the studio to write, record and release a new John Verity Band album *Routes* in 2004, feeling good to be myself again after this excursion into the education sector.

I'll always be grateful for the chance to work in education for a while, passing on my knowledge of the business and my own musical skills, and I'm proud of the many students who have gone on to success, but it never felt 100% right to be away from my first love, sure that I was always meant to get back to it one day...

Routes was a way of getting my feelings off my chest, although I suppose that's how you would describe a lot of my work, and also a vehicle to release some unfinished material, but now working alone.

'She's Not There' has always been one of my favourite Rod Argent songs and I took this opportunity to put together my own arrangement of it, playing all the instruments myself until finally asking Steve Rodford to come along and add drums for the end section.

'A Woman Like You' is a song I wrote for the first Phoenix album, and I had always wanted to try a slightly different version, so I asked Bob Henrit to come along to play drums, Mark Griffiths played bass and I played/sang everything else myself.

'Last Chance' is a blues flavoured track with lyrics written during the last period of my life, and I think it's pretty obvious what it's about, again with Bob and Mark playing drums and bass.

'Boyz' was initially recorded during the final sessions that Steve Thompson and I did together, on the same session as 'Eyes On You' included later in the album. As with 'She's Not There' I asked Steve Rodford to put drums on the tracks after everything else was recorded — a skill that very few drummers have, although Steve nailed it each time, first take!

'Waiting' was one of last tracks I recorded for *Routes*, and I did everything on this track myself, writing most of the lyric in the period when Carole and I were thinking of getting together and then finishing it off once we were settled in Cardington.

'When I'm Away from You' was initially meant to be a bit like an early sixties record but of course as I worked on it, it moved away from that into the feel you hear on the album, although I still feel it worked as a piece.

'Down The Road' is based on an idea I've worked on many times over the years, and the version on *Routes* is an early attempt, with Bob and Mark on drums and bass again.

'You're The One' is based around the initial guitar riff and I was looking for something light-hearted that might work in a live context — with Bob and Mark again.

'Dirty Old Man' came about when I was asked to submit a song for consideration by Tina Turner, and in my head I can still hear her singing it, although it wasn't accepted at the time sadly.

Once *Routes* was finished and released in 2004, I began to feel my days in education were numbered and I was ready to focus again on my music full-time, but first I had committed to complete a number of projects for Pearson.

I had contracts to visit colleges in Italy to deliver training to teachers in 2005, so Carole came with me on these trips to Bologna and Rome and enjoyed doing the tourist thing for a while before returning to her contract work at home.

Carole's next financial contract was in London where she was working on business complaints for a major bank, and it might well have been her last.

On 7th July 2005 we left early as I drove Carole to Bedford Station to catch her train to London, little knowing that when the train stopped in Luton, someone would board the train carrying a hidden bomb.

Under normal circumstances, Carole would have been on that train when the bomb went off but this particular morning, she decided on a change of plan, to get off early, as the trains were running late, and it would be quicker to walk the last part of the journey across London.

On that day four suicide bombers, including the one on the same train as Carole struck London's transport network, killing fifty-two people, and injuring many hundred's more.

I was at home with the TV on, and on seeing the news of the bombings, tried Carole's mobile number to find that there was no service on the network.

It was horrendous, sitting there watching the news reports showing more and more carnage, unable to reach Carole so I got in the car and headed south, all the while trying to get through on the phone over and over again with no success.

Suddenly, as I reached Swiss Cottage, North London, Carole's phone began ring, she was walking north through London but many of the roads were blocked off making her zigzag journey take longer to get out of danger.

We worked out roughly where she was, and I suggested she head for Chalk Farm, and I would do the same, hoping to meet up somehow, near a venue we both knew, The Roundhouse, then we lost contact again.

The drive down from Swiss Cottage to Chalk Farm was like a scene from a movie, there was a sea of people, right across the road heading north away from danger, and I was slowly picking my way through them heading south to try to find Carole, all the while trying her number again.

Eventually, I got to Chalk Farm and finally got through to Carole again, who told me she was almost at our meeting place, and then I spotted her, striding up the road towards me.

It's impossible to explain my relief as we headed north again, our luck really had held that day, and unlike too many others Carole was safe, and we were heading for home again.

I was glad when Carole's London contracts finished, and she accepted one at a bank in Aylesbury, a bit closer to home, and which was to be her final contract as we had decided to concentrate on my music career together with me doing what I always do, and Carole working in our office focusing on PR and getting gigs for the band.

With our future plans firmly in place Carole and I got on with honouring our work commitments, gradually winding them down and increasing time spent on the band.

By now the stable lineup of the JV Band was Bob Henrit on drums, with Steve Rodford occasionally stepping in, Mark Griffiths on bass, with Bob Skeat stepping in when available depending on commitments with Wishbone Ash.

Around this time, a chance meeting with Max Milligan, a brilliant guitarist from the Bedford area led to conversations between the two of us about the possibility of working together on some acoustic flavoured material.

I had already begun featuring more acoustic guitar tracks on my recorded material and some of my recent songs might really work in an acoustic context, so we decided to give it a go.

We arranged some local gigs where we would play together, having a great time with me trying to keep up with the acoustic virtuoso sitting next to me absolutely playing the arse off his poor Martin guitar — it was scary, but really good for my own technique, I was raising my game again!

At one of these gigs, guitarist Del Bromham was in the audience, and we had a brief chat in the break which would eventually lead to much more, years later...

Carole and I had formed our own record label, planning to keep everything in house from now on, alongside Verity Music' for publishing my songs, the label was called VaVoom Records, and Max agreed that we should put out a Verity/Milligan CD on VaVoom.

Unplugged and Unhinged was a perfect title for Max and I, our live shows were pretty crazy, we were just there to have a great time and play some music, so this title for our first album together seemed just right.

We recorded twelve tracks at my place, although the CD shows thirteen with a bit of frivolity I couldn't resist adding at the end.

'The One' is one of my songs that was first featured on the *Routes* album and it works really well here as an acoustic track, with our friend Jeff Dakin adding brilliant harmonica parts.

'Sweet Medicine' was sung and written by Max and mainly features Max's brilliant acoustic guitar playing, with some nice harmonica flavour from Jeff once again.

'Pride' is one of mine, I had been messing around with some alternative tunings on my guitar and this song sort of wrote itself. It was crying out for a pedal steel part, so we asked our friend Rob Bond along, and he played the beautiful pedal steel part, so important to the finished track — thanks Rob, you're a star!

'Waiting' is one of mine, again I'd done a version on *Routes* but this version includes more of a focus on the acoustic guitars, although I added a bass part to round out the bottom end.

'Wish I knew How It Would Feel To Be Free' is a piece written by Billy Taylor that was made famous as the opening music to a BBC TV film review show and had served as an anthem for the Civil Rights movement in America in the 1960s. Our version is very basic, just two guitars playing sympathetically across each other.

'6345789' is an old favourite of Max and I, and for this one we invited Richard Blackley along to play drums with us, with Mark playing bass again.

'Mess Of Blues' another old favourite, written by Pomus/Shuman and originally recorded by Elvis Presley, with Richard and Mark supporting Max and I again as we deliver our own arrangement.

'If Loving You Is Wrong' is one of my favourite songs, and this version was recorded live at one of our shows at the Crown in Northill, the very same Crown where I fell to pieces after the theft of my gear from the Tricky Truck. Mark plays a lovely, sympathetic bass part on this one.

'Song for Vicky' is a beautiful piece written and played solo by Max and it's a perfect example of Max's ability as a guitar player. Beautiful.

'Sweet Potato' was written by Booker T Jones and we recorder our version with Mark on bass and Denny McCaffrey on percussion.

'High Heel Sneakers' is another classic close to our hearts, it was one of the songs I learned early in my career and for this simple version we just have Mark on bass with Max and me.

'Gone' is one of the songs in our live set that brings a chuckle or two from the audience as Max sings the crazy John Hiatt lyric. Max added the bass on this one and I added background vocals with Max.

A spider fell from the ceiling as we did these background vocals and just missed scaredy cat Max!

Since starting our own label, we realised we needed a website to help with sales and marketing, so I approached a good friend, Marc Sinclair to help with this.

Marc had for some time been the person we would turn to with any computer problems, and I knew he was the right person to set this up for us.

Pretty soon johnverity.com was up and running, and set up nicely for information on the band, and the sale of our merchandise including CDs and T-Shirts.

Since then, Marc has also been responsible for the artwork on most of our CDs and Vinyl, coming up with great ideas of the highest quality each time.

You're a genius Marc!

The next recording project for the band was due, and for a while people had been asking us for a live album, so I booked a couple of days at our local Village Hall and announced that we would record in front of an invited audience.

All the available tickets were gone in no time at all so with Bob Henrit and Mark Griffiths we played the whole of our live set, in front of a specially invited audience of around forty people (the maximum for the small hall we were using) with short technical breaks to kick the computer we were using to record the set, into life!

The resultant album *Live 101* came out in 2006 and seemed to satisfy our fans demand for a live album and record the current band live set for posterity.

Looking back, some of the songs played that day are still in the set as I write this.

I can't be the only musician who when updating the setlist as time goes by gets complaints from fans saying "why don't you play... anymore? I really like that song can you please put it back in the show."

Well I do, and I do...

Often, I will get the germ of a song idea at the of the day, sometimes as I'm about to get into bed, and I do have a habit of sitting by the bed playing guitar for a bit before getting into bed at night.

When this noodling on guitar leads to a song idea I will often run down to the studio, which is in the room below our bedroom and either scribble the idea down on a piece of paper or record it on my phone.

One such idea came to me in the period when Max and I were first spending time together at my place working on songs for a possible live set.

When Max arrived, I was excited about a song idea that had come to me the night before, so I picked up a guitar and played a very raw version of the song to him, disappointed to see that he really wasn't impressed at all with the idea.

Embarrassed, I put the guitar down and began to focus on the work that we were doing on the JV and Max set.

The song idea that I had played to Max developed into one of my most popular pieces, 'Say Why', which has ended up being one of those songs that I just can't leave out of the JV Band show because if I do, people complain, and it has to go back in again.

I guess that often, when I scribble down, or make a rough recording of an idea it only really makes sense to me, and that much of the song is still only in my head meaning this initial attempt doesn't make sense to anyone else.

'Say Why' ended up as the title track for my album released in 2007, recorded at home with Bob Henrit playing drums and Mark

Griffiths on bass, with Gary Moberly adding keyboard parts and Jeff Dakin playing Blues Harp on 'The One'.

Although the initial idea for the song began with the intro guitar riff, which continues throughout the song, 'Say Why' is probably the first time I had put my feelings about what was going on around me, and across the world into a lyric, and I guess this is what people connect with when they hear the song.

Another song on the *Say Why* album, 'Too Hot to Hug' came about one hot summer night as I sat by the bed, trying to cool down before getting under the sheets.

I imagined a scenario where the guy came home hoping for some action with his lady, only to be told that it was 'Too Hot To Hug'.

We still play this song in the set, and I often tell the story as if it actually happened at home between Carole and me, and usually the audience is treated to Carole calling out that I'm a lying S.O.B!

2010 was a strange year in some ways, it started in a really positive way, with Max and me playing some really enjoyable shows with our acoustic set and then later Bob and I making plans for a new Phoenix album.

We had chatted about the Argent situation and come to the conclusion that Argent was gone forever, especially as Rod had hooked up with Colin Blunstone again in a partnership that would revive The Zombies.

I felt that it would be a great idea to do a Phoenix album that had a bit of an Argent flavour to it, with covers of some of the more commercial Argent songs included.

I could probably finance the project too, as I had just been approached by a Japanese record label that wanted to licence some of my back catalogue to release a box set in Japan.

I spoke to Don McKay at Rhino Agency, and he was interested on getting onboard to book shows for us, so it really looked like it was a viable project.

I secured the Japanese deal to raise the finance and booked a residential studio Grange Farm in Norfolk so that we could all stay together as we recorded the tracks, intending to take the resultant recordings home to add any finishing touches and make the final mixes.

The studio was run by Dave and Sue Williams, and was perfect for us, with a nice 'live' area, plus an excellent range of classic microphones and comfortable accommodation right there on site.

Dave is an excellent engineer and Sue the perfect host to make the visit as productive as possible.

I made contact with an old friend, Ray Staff, who used to be the mastering engineer at Trident Studios back in the original Phoenix days and asked him to master this new project at Air Studios where he was currently located.

The project was going to cost a considerable amount of money, but I felt at the time that we should do everything properly, to the highest possible quality to make the finished product something special.

The recordings were going really well, and we first put down a really nice new version of 'Say Why', with Mark adding 12-string guitar, which I hadn't had on the earlier version.

The guide vocal that I had laid down as we recorded the track worked out really well too and there was enough separation from the instruments to keep it on the final mix if I wanted to.

Next, we recorded our version of a Russ Ballard song 'Liar' that had been a huge hit in the US by Three Dog Night and was originally recorded for the first Argent album in 1970.

I had really wanted to include one of Rod Argent's songs, and we thought that 'Time Of The Season' would be a good choice so laid that down next in a form that we felt could be a standout live version.

The rest of the album was to be original material although I already had live versions of 'Hold Your Head Up' and 'God Gave Rock 'n' Roll to you' that would fit the bill perfectly.

All the basic tracks plus a few overdubs and vocals were completed in the time I had booked at Grange Farm, and Dave backed up the recordings for me to take home and work on at my place, so we bade farewell to Dave and Sue, and hit the road.

On listening to the tracks at home I was really happy with what I heard, although I could tell that keyboards were needed to make them really work so a call to the lovely Ian Gibbons was required. Ian was an amazing player, never too fancy, always adding just what a song needed without overdoing it as some players would often do. He was perfect for this project, and I was happy to find that he had time to join me in the studio to get the job done.

Ian's main band had been The Kinks for many years and now he was running an offshoot of the band, the Kast Off Kinks.

Ian played on lots of my sessions for many years and was my go-to keyboard player over a long period but sadly, he passed away on 1st of August 2019 after suffering from bladder cancer, although he never mentioned it to anyone outside his immediate family.

Once the album was finished and ready for release, we arranged a launch gig at the Cambridge Rock Festival, and I asked Ian to join Bob, Mark, and me for the gig with a view to him being in the band moving forward.

We played the festival to a great reception and came away looking forward to making future plans for the brand-new Phoenix lineup, with a good album to promote and a band that could deliver the goods, live.

So, with everything seemingly in place I was looking forward to setting up the final piece of the puzzle — sorting out a tour with the help of our agent Don McKay.

I had hugely overspent on the project, so apart from the obvious need to get the band out on the road I needed to generate some finance to recoup some of the money I had laid out, and of course the money from gigging would really help.

My call to Don McKay didn't go as I had hoped, despite being enthusiastic the last time we had spoken he was now not really engaging with me, so I asked him if there was a problem, and his reply came as a major shock.

"I'm not sure this Phoenix project is going to work now that the original lineup of Argent has reformed".

I couldn't believe what I was hearing, and why on earth hadn't Bob told me about this, knowing that I was spending large amounts of money on a project doomed to failure.

I knew for certain that Rod wouldn't have agreed to do this without a serious amount of rehearsal, so Bob must have been doing both projects at the same time at one point, I was devastated.

At first, I couldn't understand why I hadn't been invited to be involved in some way, it's my opinion that any Argent lineup would be better with me in it, in fact an Argent lineup with me and Russell in it was a total no brainer, the vocals combined with Rod and Jim would be killer!

The more I thought about it though, the more I realised that of course the marketing angle of 'the original Argent lineup' made absolute sense, and I was sure that there were lots of fans out there who would be truly excited at the idea of turning back the clock to see all the original members on stage again… good luck to the guys, it was a great idea.

Still, I was upset, felt humiliated, and disappointed, with the new Phoenix project seeming absolutely pointless now and a shit load of expense down the drain.

I couldn't get hold of Bob at first, there was no answer from his home number, or his mobile but I kept trying until finally he answered, on holiday in France. Bob had nothing to say really, and any conversation we might have had has now totally slipped my mind.

In the end I made the decision to scrap the Phoenix album, remove the two live tracks and replace them with a couple of songs I had already finished and release the album as a Verity CD called *Rise Like The Phoenix*.

I had already released a single from the Phoenix version of the album, my version of 'Stay With Me Baby' so I kept that in the catalogue but didn't really promote it, so it sort of fizzled out...

Time to move on methinks.

This Rock 'n' Roll Won't Last You Know!

24
I Get Knocked Down, But...

2011 was a year for me to pull myself back up again, although I spent much of my time working at home, working on song ideas alone.

Early in my career I was known for playing Gibson guitars, most notably a white Gibson Les Paul Custom that I played for many years including the time I was with Argent in the seventies.

More recently I had started playing Fender guitars again — I did have a lovely blue Strat, early in the sixties but now I was back with Fender again, usually a Stratocaster, and had grown comfortable with the feel and sound of these instruments.

I would always play the classic form of a Strat as designed by Leo Fender in 1952, and first sold in 1954, which had three almost identical pickups, giving a good range of sounds from the instrument. Over the years, guitarists would start to modify their Strats, and the most popular mod was to fit a humbucking pickup in place of the original, near the bridge/vibrato.

The original, single coil pickup was quite bright sounding and I guess many players wanted a fatter, more Gibson-like sound in that position.

I decided to write and record a song about these modifications, basing it around my original blue, 1962 Strat, having a tongue-in-cheek dig at those who were messing with Leo's original idea, and I called the song 'Leo Had It Right'.

I asked Steve Rodford to play drums on it, releasing it as an EP with a couple of the songs that Steve Thompson and I had written, and I made a slightly comical video to go with it to use on social media.

I gotta tell you a story, began about '62
She was such a beautiful baby, young and pretty and blue
I had to walk her home that day – it came as no surprise
My friends knew I was lost to her, they could see it in my eyes

Now you could say, in a number of ways we've been together since then
Sometimes I'd try to change here but I'd only put her back again
Take my advice, hold on, think twice don't change the one you love
Remember how it started, how she fitted you like a glove

Don't change that bridge, lower them frets or fit that new humbucker
Cos after all is said and done, you're only gonna ruin the clucker
It seems I've messed around for all of my rockin' life
But all that messin's just window dressing Cos Leo had it right.

Well now you've heard my story, you know what you must do
Go out and find your baby, and to your baby be true
She'll never let you down, don't make her change her ways
She'll stay right by your side, through all of your rockin' days.

Don't change that bridge, lower them frets or fit that new humbucker
Cos after all is said and done, you're only gonna ruin the clucker
It seems I've messed around for all of my rockin' life
But all that messin's just window dressing Cos Leo had it right.

By 2012 the JV Band was still gigging regularly, often with Bob on drums and sometimes with Steve Rodford stepping in, with bass duties still shared by Bob Skeat and Mark Griffiths although a new recruit Andy Childs was also slotting in from time to time.

It was time for a new album, and I decided to incorporate some of the acoustic feels that Max and I had been doing, into the band format this time.

I had just met Trev Wilkinson too, meaning a slight diversion in the tools I would be using to make this new music. Trev is somewhat of a Guru in guitar circles, having come up with solutions to age old problems like tuning issues, that had now been adopted by even the most traditional guitar builders.

For example Fender had begun to use Trev's 'Roller Nut' on the Stratocaster to help to improve tuning stability when using the tremolo arm, a modification welcomed by players including Jeff Beck.

Anyway, Trev and I met at a trade show in London in 2012, and after the introductions Trev said to me, "I can see you're playing a Strat — what's wrong with it?".

I laughed at first, but then realised he was serious, and told him a couple of things I didn't really like about my expensive, American made Fender Stratocaster but was just putting up with.

Trev's response was, "Why don't I build you a guitar that fixes those problems?"

Trev kept his promise, and since then all my guitars have been Trev Wilkinson designs, including my 'JV Signature' guitars, and I can't see that changing anytime soon.

On hooking up with Trev, I began to play regularly at guitar shows up and down the country to promote the JV Signature guitars and to build the brand for the company.

The shows were usually on Sunday afternoons, so didn't really get in the way of gigs as I could usually make it in time to an evening show if I had one.

I was happy to promote the product, as I believed in it, and also the shows were a good opportunity to reach a different type of audience, plus I was still taking a full band with me and the shows always had a decent stage area, and provided full P.A system, professionally organised so all was good.

Back at home equipped with my new guitars I began to record my next album, soon to be titled *It's A Mean Old Scene*.

The phrase 'It's a mean old scene' appeared as graffiti on a wall that my bus would often pass at my hometown, Bradford in the sixties and it has stuck in my mind ever since.

I thought it would make a great album title and pay homage to my background in Bradford.

The opening track has been a staple in the live show for ages, so 'Hoochie Coochie Man' went down quickly, with Steve Rodford playing drums and Bob Skeat playing bass, and this was the main lineup for the rhythm on album although the later tracks, 11-14 were added for a special edition and feature Bob Henrit again on drums.

My version of 'I'd Rather Go Blind' was picked by HBO in America for a scene in their *Sharp Objects* series, a welcome bit of publicity for the album and it generated huge streams on Spotify as a result.

Much of this album features my favourite blues standards that I felt would work with a slightly, rocky approach and I think it really works.

As planned, two acoustic tracks are included, 'Come In My Kitchen' and 'Rolling And Tumbling', each featuring Max Milligan and Jeff Dakin on guitar and blues harp respectively and this was a formula I retained for the next couple of albums.

There followed a period of heavy gigging, partly to try and get to as many people as possible across the UK and partly to generate much needed money as I was still recovering from the Phoenix album mess.

One of favourite gigs locally is the Stables Theatre, in Wavendon, Milton Keynes, only twenty minutes from home, where there are two rooms, our favourite being The Jim Marshall Auditorium.

Jim Marshall of course is the man responsible for the world-famous Marshall amplifier that I have used on and off for the last fifty years or more, since I bought my first Marshall stack in the 1960s. I knew Jim quite well, and we last met in 2011 when the 'Father of Loud' came to see me at an acoustic show that Max and I were doing close to his home in Milton Keynes, not long before he passed away in 2012.

Jim was a great supporter of the musicians who used his gear and always made sure that we could drop our amps in to the Bletchley factory for service to keep them working to their full potential at reasonable cost.

R.I.P. Jim, thanks for everything.

Whenever we play theatre or festival shows, merchandise plays a big part in spreading the word and keeping the band viable financially, and Carole takes care of this, in addition to booking our gigs and dealing with promotion.

Carole often needs a helping hand at our shows, and one of my dearest friends, Lynne Birrell has been there to support her so many times over recent years that I've lost count.

Lynne and I first met in the late sixties when I was with The Richard Kent Style. She's a true music fan, a great supporter of live music around her hometown of Newcastle upon Tyne, and always there to support us through thick and thin, and seeing all the peaks and troughs in my personal and professional life over the years.

I'm not really so good at expressing my gratitude but I do truly appreciate the way that Lynne has always stayed such a good friend — she must have wondered what on earth was I doing at various points in this crazy journey but has never judged me.

Thank you, Lynne, from the bottom of my heart.

The lineup of the JV band in this period was pretty stable with Bob Henrit back for most shows, and either Steve Rodford or John Clark filling in when Bob wasn't available.

In between gigs, I was spending as much time as possible in the studio writing and recording for my next album, with Bob taking on most of the drum duties, Bob Skeat or Mark Griffiths on bass, and Ian Gibbons on keyboards.

As with the last album, I decided to include a couple of acoustic, blues flavoured tracks and asked Max to join me again, with Robbie Stuart-Mathews on blues harp as we recorded 'Help Me' and 'Everyday I Have The Blues' live in the studio.

Instead of doing all the vocals myself on this one, I asked Bianca Kinane to feature on lead vocals for two tracks, 'Would You' and 'Touch My Soul' and also asked her to join me on the background vocals across the rest of the album.

'Would You' was written by Vivienne Boucherat, who along with husband Chris White contributed some amazing backing vocal parts across the album, and 'Touch My Soul' was written by Michael Fennelly for his 1974 album *Lane Changer*.

Lane Changer was produced by Chris White and 'Touch My Soul' was, for me, the standout track on the album, one of those songs that over the years keep popping back into my head until in the end I can't resist doing my own version…

As usual I produced the album but was ably assisted on these two tracks by Chris and Viv, so the album credits rightly reflect this.

Bianca, and her keyboard playing friend and colleague Tom Wilson also joined us for selected live shows, including The Stables delivering those beautiful vocals on the songs we'd recorded and some nice arrangements of songs like 'I Just Wanna Make Love To You'.

The completed album, titled *Tone Hound On The Last Train To Corona* was released in 2014, and the opening track, my arrangement of Jay Hawkins' 'I Put A Spell On You' is one of the songs that remains in the JV Band live set to this day.

One of my songs for this album 'Too Much – Much Too Young' had me thinking about the entitlement shown by some of the young people I seemed to be coming across, sadly too often.

Too Much – Much Too Young

It's a tricky situation, it's a fine line
One more conversation, it's the ultimate crime
It's the choice that you made, but you made the wrong choice
You can hear yourself screaming
But no-one hears your voice

You had too much, much too young
You had too much, and now the damage is done
You had too much, too much time
You went too far, now it's the end of the line

Too many complications, it's a cruel world
Despite all our conversations, you didn't get it girl
People get tired, people get mean
You're full of what you heard, full of what you've seen
People get mad, people get sad
How come it came to this after everything you had?

You had too much, much too young
You had too much, and now the damage is done
You had too much, too much time
You went too far, now it's the end of the line
(John Verity, Verity Music)

On a much lighter note, one of the other songs I wrote for this album 'Nothing's Changed', came about when one day I was watching my lovely, better half, Carole realising how strong our relationship was after all these years and how my feelings for her are as strong as ever.

Nothing's Changed

I see my baby walking down the street
She's still the kind of girl I'd like to meet
Nothing's changed, nothing's changed
She's still my sweet little angel, nothing's changed

I hold my baby and I have to say
She's still one who takes my breath away
Nothing's changed, nothing's changed
She's still my sweet little angel, nothing's changed

She's my walking talking hugging kissing moving grooving work of art
I still remember when we met you know she stole my heart
That was the start

I see my baby and she looks so good
She looks exactly like I hoped she would
Nothing's changed, nothing's changed
She's still my sweet little angel, nothing's changed

She's my walking talking hugging kissing moving grooving work of art
I still remember when we met you know she stole my heart
That was the start

I see my baby and she looks so good
She looks exactly like I hoped she would
Nothing's changed, nothing's changed
She's still my sweet little angel, nothing's changed

I hold my baby and I have to say
She's still one who takes my breath away
Nothing's changed, nothing's changed
She's still my sweet little angel, nothing's changed

(John Verity, Verity Music)

As Christmas approached, I had a crazy idea that I should record a Christmas CD and asked Bob to pop up to the studio to lay some tracks.

Many of my favourite artists had been encouraged (forced?) by their record labels to record Christmas singles over the years and I fancied recording some tongue-in-cheek versions myself for a bit of a laugh, although also it might generate a bit of interest.

My idea was to just record four songs for a Christmas EP – 'Merry Christmas Baby', 'Santa Claus Is Back In Town', 'Run Rudolph Run' and 'Blue Christmas', all with a sort of blues/rock feel.

Bob and I laid down the drums, guitar, and vocal parts together and I added the bass guitar later, leaving all the songs really stripped down just as if we were playing them live for our hard-core of fans and it turned out to be a really popular idea. Daft but popular!

After a short break for the holiday we were back out on the road again and I was thinking about my next recording project.

I really wanted to do something old-school with everyone in the studio together like we used to do it, and a good friend Rob Bond had just finished building a studio with a live area big enough to set up the whole band, together.

It was possible to do this at home of course but I really wanted to concentrate on playing guitar for a change and let someone else worry about recording it!

I booked a couple of days at Rob's place, called Bosky Studio, planning to get a few tracks down, and then bring the recordings home to finish and mix them, calling it a 'live in the studio album'.

I wanted to get Bianca on the album too but would record her at my place as she had commitments on the days I'd booked at Rob's place. Bianca would travel down with her keyboard playing musical partner Tom Wilson again as before.

On the first day in the studio, we just basically got our gear in, set up and got all the sounds and headphone balances right, intending to come in fresh the next day to begin recording.

On the second day, Bob Henrit, Bob Skeat and myself put down seven tracks with Rob at the controls, just having a good time playing material we were familiar with, as I wasn't really interested in recording new material at this time.

We did a new version of my song 'Nothing's Changed' and a nice, live version of 'Say Why'.

I wanted Bianca to sing 'I just wanna make love to you' so we laid that down, having first checked what key she wanted to sing it in.

'I Put A Spell On You' was an obvious choice for a live version. We jammed around on 'The Blues Had A Baby And They Named It Rock & Roll' and it worked out really well.

'Route 66' went down in double quick time and brought back lots of great memories as we used to play it together many years earlier.

'Johnny B Goode' was a bit of a no brainer for what was essentially a jam session, and then we packed up and headed for home.

For the actual CD I added a couple of 'bonus tracks' that I already had, recorded as demos at my place, 'While My Guitar Gently Weeps' with Bianca singing lead vocal, and 'Help Me', which I was just about to add to our live set.

The CD came out early in 2015, with nine tracks in total.

Later in 2015, due to the success of the first Christmas CD I decided to do another one, recorded in the same way as the first one with Bob and I but this time I'd found some songs that I hadn't been aware of before.

I discovered that even my favourite blues artists had had their arms twisted into making Christmas records.

'Trim Your Tree' is a slightly risqué song first recorded by Jimmy Butler.

'Santa Claus Got The Blues' was recorded by The Drifters.

'Santa Claus Wants Some Loving Tonight' was first recorded by none other than Albert King!

'Please Come Home For Christmas' originally by blues pianist Charles Brown.

And finally, 'Back Door Santa' by BB King.

So with tongue firmly in cheek again Bob and I recorded the tracks, and again I added the bass guitar part afterwards. There was a bit more 'production' applied this time as I added some backing vocals, although apart from that the finished article is pretty basic.

Onward and upward...

We market most of my CDs on Amazon, and Spotify, as well as directly from my website, and I was checking our inventory on Spotify one day when an album came up that I didn't recognise — *John Verity Plays His Favourite Led Zeppelin Tracks*.

I certainly didn't remember releasing this album, and when I checked it was pretty obvious that whoever had released it had lifted all the photos and art from my website!

It didn't look as though this release was actually on CD, it was just being released through Spotify, so I contacted them and made a complaint against the record company involved.

Pretty soon I received a letter from a German lawyer saying that his client had a licence for the product, which I knew couldn't be true and, in any case, they didn't have my permission to use my name.

I pointed this out in my reply and demanded to see their license but then noticed when I scrolled down that the lawyer was inadvertently leaving the whole email trail intact below our conversations. Interesting, especially when I saw that the clients first response when the lawyer told him of my complaint was "just tell him to fuck off"!

So, I waited for the lawyer's response, and when it arrived, I scrolled down to see what their conversation looked like.

It was very enlightening, to say the least, as when the client had responded telling his lawyer that his license seemed to have 'expired', the lawyer warned him that they needed to be very careful as if Spotify upheld my complaint, it would be a 'third strike'.

Apparently, Spotify have strict rules, and this label was in danger of having their whole catalogue removed from the streaming service due to repeated breaches of the rules.

Clearly this guy was a crook.

The lawyer was advising his client to quickly make me an offer of payment for damages, followed by the removal of the offending recordings.

I accepted the offer, and the album did indeed disappear from Spotify, and at that point I decided to release my own album using the same Zeppelin recordings that I'd made years earlier, calling my album *Zep it Up!*

Time to move on to some new recordings.

I had spent some time writing for a new album and hoped to have it ready in time for the next Stables show as the project I was planning was likely to be expensive and required a 'proper' launch event.

I wanted to release an album on vinyl as well as CD this time, and this would be expensive and required some serious thought in order to raise the money to fund it. There are of course lots of ways to raise funding, but I decided to go it alone and throw it out to fans to help, in return for some special, career-related 'treasures' that I had collected over the years.

With this in mind I pressed on in the studio, aiming to make my best album so far in a technical sense, whilst satisfying the resurgent market for vinyl, it was exciting and daunting at the same time.

I remember being really happy with the selection of songs I had ready for the project, and I felt that one of them, 'My Religion' would also be a good title for the album.

One slight complication at the outset was running time, as the songs I wanted to use far exceeded the length that could be fitted onto a vinyl disc, so a double album would have to be budgeted for.

I knew that for the vinyl quality I was aiming for, ideally each side of the album should be about twenty-two minutes, and forty-four minutes on a CD those days wouldn't have been acceptable to some, so double vinyl, with a nice long CD was what I would aim for.

I ended up with ten tracks on the album, six of my own songs, and four covers of songs that I felt fitted in nicely with the feel of the album as a whole.

I wanted Bianca to feature again, and 'Chain Of Fools' was a perfect vehicle for her wonderful voice, backed by a new arrangement fitting the JV Band approach.

I had also written a new song, 'Farkhunda', that had a vocal part I felt was perfect for Bianca.

Whilst in a hotel room, I think in Germany, watching the BBC World Service I saw a piece that hit me right between the eyes, the heartbreaking story of an Afghan lady called Farkhunda.

Farkhunda Malikzada was a 27-year-old Afghan woman who was lynched by a mob in Kabul on 19th March 2015. She was murdered after allegedly arguing with a mullah who falsely accused her of burning the Quran, the holy book of Islam, although police investigations revealed that she had not burned anything.

Farkhunda had been arguing with the mullah named Zainuddin, in front of a mosque where she worked as a religious teacher, about his practice of selling charms promising to help women to become pregnant. According to eyewitnesses, hundreds of angry civilians flocked to the mosque upon hearing the mullah's accusation, and they dragged Farkhunda out, kicked and beat her before throwing her from a roof.

She was then run over by a car.

The mob then set her body alight and dragged it to the Kabul River, while police looked on.

A number of prominent public officials turned to Facebook

immediately after the death, to endorse the murder. The official spokesman for the Kabul police Hashmat Stanekzai, for instance, wrote that Farkhunda "thought like several other unbelievers, that this kind of action and insult will get them U.S. or European citizenship, but before reaching their target they lost their life".

Farkhunda

Farkhunda, a hero in our eyes
In a culture built on lies, yet another sacrifice
Farkhunda
They'll never know 'The Truth'
You reasoned – there's no use
There was nothing you could do

Farkhunda
I still hear, your mother's tears
Your sister's fears
Farkhunda
They failed you
Now we're crying too, what good will that do?

Farkhunda
They violate your faith
You were so far away, Farkhunda, Farkhunda
Farkhunda, your spirit, and their lies
Will stay with me, 'til I die
The only question Why?

Farkhunda
I still hear, your mother's tears
Your sister's fears
Farkhunda
They failed you
Now we're crying too, what good will that do?

(John Verity, Verity Music)

Zalmai Zabuli, chief of the complaints commission of the upper house of parliament, posted a picture of Farkhunda with this message: "This is the horrible and hated person who was punished by our Muslim compatriots for her action".

The Deputy Minister for Culture and Information Simin Ghazal Hasanzada also approved of the execution of a woman "working for the infidels".

After it was revealed that she did not burn the Quran, the public reaction turned to shock and anger. Hundreds of protesters took to the streets of Kabul on 23rd March protesting her brutal death, marching from where the attack began to where Farkhunda was thrown onto the riverbed.

A number of women on the march wore masks of her bloodied face.

On 22nd March, a number of women, dressed in black, carried Farkhunda's coffin from an ambulance to a prayer ground and then to a graveyard.

This was a marked departure from tradition, which holds that such funerals are typically only attended by men.

I made a video to accompany the track, and posted in on YouTube, expecting abuse but got none.

The song 'My Religion' is a tongue in cheek, less than subtle dig at organised religion, but I feel that 'Farkhunda' demonstrates the evil that can also come with religious beliefs.

At the outset, I hadn't intended to write a song like 'Farkhunda' for this album, preferring instead to poke fun if you will, but the day I saw the BBC piece on the Farkhunda story mine became a song I just had to write, and it probably changed the whole feel of the album if the listener can be bothered to really listen.

The rest of the album went pretty much as planned and I did manage to raise the finance to go ahead with the vinyl, gatefold double disc version with excellent artwork created by Marc Sinclair, probably my best work so far.

When it came to manufacture of the vinyl version, I did have some shocks to contend with though... As I mentioned previously, I had recorded the whole album at very high sample rates to get the best I could from the vinyl version, and when the time came, I began to approach companies who deal with vinyl manufacture.

The first company I approached gave me the price I had hoped for, but when I asked them what format they wanted the audio files in they simply said, "oh just send us a CD!"

I couldn't believe it — all the work I had put into the album, and they were going to cut the vinyl version from CD, which was vastly inferior to the quality of my masters.

Subsequent calls revealed that this seemed to be common practice, meaning there must be an awful lot of vinyl out there that has been manufactured in this way, I wonder what the people who bought this inferior product would think if they knew the truth?

I decided to go to my friend Ray Staff at Air Studios to have the vinyl 'parts' made, so that I could be in control of the process.

Air Studios have all the classic disc cutting equipment including an original Neumann cutting lathe, so at the end of the day I headed for home with the best quality resources to allow my chosen manufacturer to get my album to me the way I wanted it.

I now have it on authority that this scandalous method of manufacturing vinyl from CD is a thing of past.

Once we had stock of the CDs and vinyl for *My Religion* it was time to find an outlet in addition to our usual practice of selling at gigs, Amazon and my website.

I was introduced to Steve Rossi, a vinyl aficionado involved in a record store on the south coast, and he agreed to stock our album. Steve was and is also somewhat of a social media expert and was about to become involved with us more closely as we explored new ways to promote the JV Band and our merchandise, through his company Rossi's Social Media.

Reaction to the *My Religion* album was excellent, and the launch show at the Stables went really well, with new tracks from the album also working well in the new live set.

'My Religion'. 'Hope For The Best', and 'Prove Your Love' stayed in the JV Band show for quite a while, following their debut and as before at the Stables I invited Bianca and Tom to join us, so that we could feature 'Chain Of Fools' with Bianca's vocal intact, as on the album version.

I was beginning to feel that Bob was losing interest in playing drums with me.

The clues were pretty obvious really, Bob didn't seem to be getting behind the new material I'd written in the way he usually would, and at gigs he would be a little detached from me.

Bob and I had been really close for over forty years, it hurt that our friendship seemed to be fading after all this time and I couldn't really work out what was going on.

Because Bob had recently been working with Russ Ballard, who had decided to go back on the road again, I thought perhaps that was part of it, as Bob and Russ had known each other for even longer, since The Roulettes, Adam Faith and Unit 4+2 days when they first began playing music together. There must have been a lot of new material for Bob to learn for Russ, as well as my stuff so maybe that was part of it.

There did seem to be a bit of light at the end of the tunnel though, when Russ called me to suggest I joined his band for the current tour meaning that Bob and I would be working together in Russ's band.

A chance to 'mend fences'.

I spoke to Russ's manager to discuss the possibilities and was pleased to find that Russ's tour dates didn't actually clash with any JV Band dates meaning I could do both.

We arranged that I would do my first date with Russ at the Giants Of Rock Festival on 30th January 2016, having played the night before with my own band.

Bob had told me he was going to be unavailable for a few JV Band gigs due to his commitments with Russ, and I had found someone to take his place, a brilliant young drummer, Liam James Gray.

Liam did his first show with me on 23rd January 2016, at Leo's Red Lion in Gravesend, and he played brilliantly, so I was confident that my band would continue safely while Bob was unavailable, and that I'd have cover moving forward too.

Liam would play with my band on the 29th January at Giants Of Rock, and catch a train home, while I stayed over to do the 30th show with Russ.

I was to be replacing the current guitarist in Russ's band, who had decided to cease touring due to illness, but for this first gig he was playing the bulk of the show, with me coming on for the last few numbers, when Russ would introduce me as the new member of his band.

I had learned the guitar parts for the songs Russ wanted me to play, and also any harmony vocals that were needed. Russ would call me on from the wings when it was time for to join him.

As we got ready in the dressing room before the show Russ came to me and changed the plan, he had decided to change the set and I would come on later, doing less songs.

No problem, I was perfectly happy with that but as I stood in the wings watching the show, I was shocked to be called on earlier, especially as I was standing there with no guitar — it was back in the dressing room!

I ran to the dressing room, grabbed my guitar, and ran back to the stage but they were now playing the song without me, so I stood out of sight waiting for a cue to go on stage later.

Russ called me and introduced me before going into the intro for 'Since You Been Gone', one of the songs I was due to play and at last we were off and running, except when it came to the second verse Russ pointed across at me to sing the lead vocal.

Shit, I wasn't expecting this, I didn't know the words for the verse and proceeded to make up new words as I sang, until Russ realised what was going on and took over from me.

Not a great start, but nobody in the audience seemed to notice and we completed the set to a great reaction from the crowd and left the stage.

Clearly, I was going to have to learn all the words in case it happened again!

A few days later, myself and everyone in Russ's band received an email from his manager, telling us to 'stand down' as the tour dates were about to be changed, a minor disaster as we all had other commitments.

Sure enough, when the new dates came through, many of them clashed with JV Band shows, meaning I would be unavailable for Russ's dates as I was determined to honour the commitment I had made to my own shows, and band members. I responded to Russ's manager, telling him the dates I could, and couldn't do, but Russ was unhappy, called me and said it would have to be all the shows or none at all.

I told Russ it would have to be none at all, and the call ended abruptly. Russ and I have remained friends, this was just a bit of a hiccup, although I still wish I'd had the opportunity to tour with him.

I continued my shows with the JV Band, and Liam was making a great job of it, with Bob doing less and less of my gigs until eventually he wasn't doing any.

Our relationship went through a really rough patch, although as I write this things are fine again, we chat regularly on the phone and

Bob spends most of his time focusing on his writing, having pushed the live gigging to one side.

I'm grateful for our lasting friendship, despite its ups and downs, although I hope I won't be asking Bob to be my 'Best Man' again anytime soon!

This Rock 'n' Roll Won´t Last You Know!

25
All Change

The band seemed to be entering a new phase now, with new members entering the ever-changing lineup. Liam was now firmly in the driving seat when it came to drum duties although Steve Rodford was occasionally filling in.

Wishbone Ash seemed to be doing a lot more work meaning that Bob Skeat wasn't as free to work with us as he had been before, so I had been drawing from a pool of good people with the time to help.

Very few gigging musicians seem to stick with one band these days as they search for enough work to survive so I have to find the right people as, and when, the gigs come in.

Jamie Mallender and Gav Coulson, both excellent players based in the North were helping me out, Jamie played on 'Devils Music' on the *My Religion* album, and John Gordon was doing a lot of the Southern dates.

Derek White would also take on bass duties at times when available although we had a new contender for the permanent bass seat in the band, Roger Inniss.

Roger is simply brilliant, an amazing bassist, lovely bloke, and a great personality on stage, really popular with audiences everywhere. I took to Roger immediately, both musically and personally, and as I began writing for the next album it seemed natural to invite him to the studio to provide many of the bass parts.

Steve Rossi was either helping Carole to do our social media stuff or was doing it for us until we were proficient enough to take it on, and he would sometimes be at our gigs to help with the PR aspect of what we were doing.

For the next album I had decided to have a mix of old and new in terms of approaches to material, as the JV Band had shifted a little over the years, back and forth across the rock, soul, and blues genre.

The first song I wrote for this album was 'Such A Feeling', and I wanted to record it in the style of my eighties albums, *Interrupted Journey* and *Truth Of The Matter* and open the album with it.

Such A Feeling

Out on the road, comin' alive
Out on the road, you by my side
Ready or not, give it all we've got
Come on, let's go

Such a Feeling, here in my heart
Such a Feeling, keep moving, keep moving on...

Out on the road, brothers in arms
Out on the road, the way I like it
Gotta steal the show, everywhere we go
Come on, get ready let's go

Such a Feeling, here in my heart
Such a Feeling, keep moving, keep moving on...

(John Verity, Verity Music)

Bob Skeat played bass on this one, with Hammond organ parts played by Jamie Pipe.
I layered up all the backing vocals myself, the way I used to do back in the day.

The second track on the album, 'This Old Dog' was another one intended for the live set, and Jamie Pipe played Hammond organ again, with Roger Innis playing bass.

Next up is 'Blues In Heaven' written for my old friend Mally Jackson, who sadly was seriously ill, and soon to pass away.

I managed to finish the album before Mally died, and he requested this track and got it played on *Planet Rock* radio, bless him. R.I.P Mally, old buddy.

Roger played bass on this one, with Jamie on organ again.

'Blues Is My Business' is my cover of a song first recorded by Etta James, and it was already in our live set, so I wanted to have a recorded version available.

Roger on bass, with Bob Fridzema on piano, and Jamie on organ.

I first heard 'Never Gonna Change' by Buddy Guy and felt such an affinity with the lyric that I just had to record it. Jamie Mallender played bass with Ian Gibbons on keyboards.

'Alabama' was recorded simply, with Max on guitar as before, as I wanted to include a traditional blues in a raw form. I think it works.

'Say The Word' features John Gordon on bass. I knew he'd have the kind of feel I was looking for on this song, and Bianca and I did the soulful backing vocals.

'Wasted Years' is a song that's been in my head for so long I can't remember when it started, but I finally finished it for inclusion here. Roger on bass, with me doing everything else.

The idea for 'A Better Way' came as the result of watching news reports on the conflicts we seem to see so often these days, both at home and across the world.

It's hard not to feel helpless at times.

Finally, I had a live recording of 'Hold Your Head Up' from one of our shows at The Stables and really didn't want to waste it as it was such a true representation of the band in a live setting.

Liam James Gray on drums and Bob Skeat on bass seemed a great way to close the album.

I named the album *Blue To My Soul*, restricted it to CD this time, as to be honest vinyl sales were sadly turning out to be impractical for us. Perhaps all the reports of a resurgence in vinyl sales are a little exaggerated?

The album, in its CD form has proved to be popular with our fans, so we appear to be doing something right, and the JV Band remains a happy ship as we hit the road once again.

The 'Rock Classic Allstars' project is run by Heinz and Anke Heinemann in Bochum, Germany, and my old buddy Jeff Brown has been featuring in their concerts for some time.

Each concert consists of a 'house band' of excellent German musicians who will back up a series of guests and play a set of their own stuff.

The shows can last anything up to five hours in total, often featuring a key member from a name UK band, and this is why Jeff had first become involved, as he had previously been a member of Sweet.

I was invited because of my former membership of Argent, even though Argent hadn't been particularly big in Germany, I guess Jeff had told them I would put on a good show anyway!

The shows were structured a bit like an old-fashioned package tour, in two halves, and each guest would perform up to four songs in each half, with a tightly structured running order to avoid any delays between acts, all using the same backup band.

In order to make me feel comfortable, Jeff played bass for me, and the venues were always large, with mostly sell-out audiences.

The deal for the guest artists was a flat fee, plus a ticket for air travel, and hotel accommodation but I wanted to take Carole with me so was given cash instead of the air ticket, planning to drive across instead, using Eurostar.

I remember the first time I made one of these trips we arrived at the gig to be met by Hells Angels type security crew.

After the long drive I was thirsty, so I asked where the beer was, to be told that, "The English aren't allowed to drink yet".

It seems that the English musicians were apt to get a little bit out of order before the shows, so the promoter had decided to clip our wings a little!

Disappointed, I thought it wouldn't be too long before I would get my beer and proceeded to get my guitars and equipment ready for the show — the other reason for driving to the show instead of flying was to carry all my own equipment in the van instead of bringing a bare minimum on the plane.

Once I was set up and ready, I was shown to my dressing room, which had a huge, glass fronted cooler cabinet stocked with beer and other goodies, but my guide informed me again that the English still weren't allowed to drink, but that the band were ready for my soundcheck.

I made my way to the stage, introduced myself to the guys in the band and got on with the job in hand.

It turned out to be a very swift soundcheck, as the others had done their homework really well, and knew my material better than me! A brilliant set of musicians.

Once backstage I began to bump into familiar faces also on the bill, including Gary Moberly, former Bee Gees keyboard player who had also played on some of my recordings, Steve Whalley, who had been with Slade for some time, and of course Jeff Brown from Sweet.

This was the way these shows were structured, with a 'house band' of excellent German musicians, and a number of UK guests interspersed with popular German acts.

On subsequent visits I was featured alongside diverse artists such as John Lawton from Uriah Heep, and Doctor And The Medics, and was never surprised at this diversity as it always seemed to work well.

Another unusual aspect of these shows is that I never actually chose my own setlist, although I was allowed to influence it if I didn't like the suggestions, and this sometimes led to me doing stuff that I'd never played live before — quite challenging you could say!

The next trip involved a number of shows, with gaps in between so Carole and I drove across to the first one, leaving behind, at the Heinemann's house, our merchandise and some equipment before driving home, and flying back and forth for the next shows until the final one, when we drove across once more to retrieve our merchandise and drive home after the show.

This Rock 'n' Roll Won't Last You Know!

26
A Shock On The Horizon

I began work on my next album in 2019, oblivious to what was in store for us. I had decided to do this one the same way I had recorded back in the day, when Bob Henrit and I would lay down the basic tracks together, but this time it would be with Liam.

My friends Lee Cave-Berry and Kimberley Rew had kindly offered to let me have a couple of days at their studio, Remote Farm free of charge, a fully equipped setup with an excellent range of classic gear and a brilliant house engineer, Steve Stewart.

Prior to our sessions at Remote Farm, Liam and I made demos of the songs at my place and in a space at my next-door neighbours Sam and Mark Womack's house to get the arrangements nice and tight, making it easy to lay down really good drum and guide guitar parts easily in the time we had at our disposal with Steve Stewart.

I then brought these recordings home and proceeded to work on them in my own comfort zone, laying down my guitar parts and vocals before asking Roger and Skeaty to add their bass parts, and once again Jamie Pipe for keyboards.

I decided to release this one on CD and vinyl, but this time I would structure each track to a time limit that would make it work on a single vinyl disc, unlike *My Religion* which had required a very expensive double-disc package.

Once again, I asked Marc Sinclair to come up with concept, and prepare the artwork for the whole package.

This time there would be no cover versions of my favourite songs as before, as I had decided that it was time for an album of my own work.

I had written material drawing from influences all the way through my career, covering the genre that had coloured my musical thinking right from the start, including Blues, Rock 'n' Roll, and classic Rock.

The first track, 'Higher' is a rock track that could well have been included on one of my eighties albums.

'Wise Up' was a sort of protest song commenting on the political situation in the U.S at that time.

'Sand In My Pocket' is about the financial obstacle's faced by musicians the world over, although with tongue firmly in cheek again.

'Broken Heart' is my comment on what we are doing to our planet, a protest song if you will.

'Big Stick' is another tongue in cheek commentary, but this time aimed at politicians from both sides of the Atlantic.

'Red Devil' was my tribute to one of my musical heroes, recently deceased drummer Ginger Baker.

'Bad Boy' is my ode to another one of my heroes, Chuck Berry.

Finally, a track that I never intended to release to the public. 'The Open Road' was really just an instrumental idea that I was messing with for my own entertainment, but Carole insisted that it shouldn't be wasted like that, and that it ought to be on the album.

Who am I to argue? It has emerged as one of the most popular tracks on the album.

I finished the album, *Passion* in time to get it manufactured for release in January 2020, although the official release date was at our show at the Tivoli Theatre, Wimborne, Dorset, on 14th March, the first date of a UK-wide tour to promote *Passion*.

We had designed and bought new T-Shirts for the tour, rehearsed the new material thoroughly, and leased a new vehicle from Mercedes so we were up and running, raring to go.

We played the Tivoli gig to an enthusiastic audience and headed north after the show, intending to break our journey by spending the night at a hotel in Birmingham before striking out early next morning for Dumfries, Scotland for our slot at the Dumfries Festival.

The word 'Pandemic' was by now becoming familiar to us and people across the world, and as we travelled north it was the main subject of our conversation in the van.

We drove up to the Holiday Inn Express, Fort Dunlop, near Birmingham in the pouring rain long after midnight to find the gates locked and no clue as to how to open them.

Tired and stressed, we eventually found someone to help, parked the van safely and decamped to our rooms for some sleep, rising early the next morning for our journey to Scotland.

There wasn't a great deal of conversation as we snaked up the M6 motorway, the news on the radio, and on social media was bleak, with reports of hospital admissions due to Covid-19 reported across the world. It was a scary time.

As we reached Dumfries there was already talk of precautions, and the need to restrict contact with others, making us really uncomfortable as friendly Scots were keen to shake hands or hug us as they recognised us as one of the acts on the bill.

We knew many of the other acts playing that day, and everyone was worried, partly about the situation at the gig but also about what was going on across the country, and how it was going to affect our careers.

We focused on our usual routine, getting the gear into the venue and onto the stage ready for our show, with Carole setting up the merchandise stall, getting ready to sell, although we were all apprehensive about handing the contact with people properly.

I was also worried about Carole being in the thick of the audience while we played. The show went well, we promoted the album as planned and cleared the stage for the next band, as Carole packed up her wares ready for the long trip home.

We bade farewell to our friends, although again had the uncomfortable situation with over-friendly audience members to contend with, as no-one seemed to be aware of the current health risks, happy to shake hands and hug as before.

At last, safe in the van we headed south.

As with the earlier drive we were soon listening to concerning news on the radio, and it seemed that a total lockdown might be on the way.

Apart from the safety aspect I was also worried about our financial situation, as this tour was vital to us being able to recoup the money we'd spent, and sometimes owed, for CDs. Vinyl, T-shirts, and the lease on the van.

A disaster was looming.

We had a five-hour drive ahead, but a couple of hours into the drive I was beginning to feel unwell, hot, and sweaty and light-headed.

I was driving the van and usure as to whether I should say anything to the others, worried in case my driving might be affected but also in case I'd caught the virus — surely not?

As we drove, Carole's phone had been receiving messages from venues and promotors, cancelling upcoming shows, the tour was falling apart and I felt myself feeling worse, but battled on not wanting to add to our worries.

We paused at a service area, giving me a chance to get some fresh air and to pull myself together, although I really was feeling rough.

Back on the road the calls and messages on Carole's phone continued, and by the time we were turning off the motorway on the final stretch we had no tour left.

When we got to Cardington, I told the guys before they got into their cars that I was unwell, although no-one else seemed to be feeling any ill effects other than tiredness, and we agreed to stay in touch before parting company.

It was late, so we unloaded the van and got ready for bed, exhausted.

I woke the next morning feeling really rough, so Carole called our doctor, explaining the symptoms to be told it was probably a panic attack due to my reaction to all the work being cancelled, he would send a prescription to the pharmacy.

I started taking the prescribed medication right away, but by next morning was in a really bad way, feeling much worse and on the point of collapse.

Carole called 'Emergency' and an ambulance arrived soon after, with two paramedics who quickly began running tests to try to find the problem.

They asked Carole to explain what had happened, and what medication had the doctor prescribed?

Almost at once they knew what the problem was, and said they needed to get me to the hospital at once, as the medication I had been given had lowered my blood pressure to dangerous levels and they couldn't treat it at home.

On the ambulance ride to the hospital I could hear tracks from *Passion* playing in the drivers cab — they had a copy of the CD, I wasn't hallucinating!

Sitting in casualty surrounded by people, knowing that there was a Pandemic wasn't exactly reassuring but at least I was getting the treatment I needed, and after a few hours on a drip I was feeling much better, grateful to our NHS for sorting me out.

Carole and I returned home much later, relieved to be over this but not looking forward to trying to pick up the pieces of our shattered tour with all it's implications, it was a disaster.

The Lockdown was enforced on 25th March 2020, and it marked the beginning of an unwelcomed rest from work for us and many across the UK.

I tried to get financial help from the Government only to find that I was one of those self-employed people not eligible, although luckily as I'm a Musicians Union member I was eligible for a little from the Musicians Benevolent Fund. Not a great deal, but it helped.

Over the next few months, like many we survived by selling things that I hoped never to sell, like my treasured 1964 Gibson Firebird guitar.

I approached Mercedes, asking them to take back the van and cancel the lease but they refused, simply quoting the clauses in the contract that stipulated that the lease could not be shortened. I will never deal with Mercedes again.

Time to pick myself up and find a solution, I wondered if I could make money live streaming on Facebook, and I explored another possibility, Patreon.

Patreon is marketed as a way for creators to reach their fan base, offering a range of memberships to fans prepared to pay for different levels of direct contact, and the opportunity to buy from a range of special offers.

In setting up my Patreon account, I was concerned that, for example a £10 membership could in fact end up costing more, as Patreon seemed to then add their own 'extras'. I really didn't like this, so abandoned the Patreon idea in favour of setting up something myself.

'JV Backstage' soon became available via my website, offering different tiers of membership depending on what 'patrons' would receive in return for their contribution.

For example supporters could donate £2 per month to simply help me, receiving nothing in return except my thanks, whilst silver, gold and platinum members paying on a sliding scale would have access to increasing levels of access to videos, photos, live streams, and regular Zoom sessions with me.

The idea generated a regular hardcore of contributors, and as well as generating much needed income, created a small group of like-minded people giving support to each other through what was an extremely difficult time as the Pandemic took hold.

This group has continued to this day, my contributors have become friends, and as I write I am also making plans for my upcoming live stream.

Those reading this will have their own memories of the next few months, some tragic, and I'm truly thankful that my own family and friends came through unscathed physically although I know that many were scarred mentally, still recovering even now.

'Long Covid' is a brand-new phrase we live with and hopefully with time we'll be able to leave that behind too, as our medical professionals search for answers.

By the end of August 2020 there seemed to be some movement on the live music front, and I was asked to do a show at a 'Mini Festival' in Brampton, near Huntingdon, an outdoor event promising to be run safely in view of recent Lockdown rules.

I accepted the gig and recruited Liam and Roger to play our first show for months, an exciting but scary prospect as we might be just a little 'rusty', under the circumstances.

On the day, we arrived to find a really professional setup, in the large garden of a pub, with proper staging, and with excellent PA and lighting provided by Neil Segrott, a well-respected sound engineer based in Leicester.

The area from the front of the stage area, back towards the pub and parking area was strictly organised with large tables, spaced out safely for each group, and table service for drinks was provided.

All good so far, and the show went well, with any worries we had about being 'rusty' disappearing once we started playing together.

After the show, we packed up and loaded the van which I'd parked right next to the stage, and made our way around the site to leave, shocked to see that the area at the rear of the site was crammed with drinkers clearly oblivious to the still present need to be careful.

I decided on that day to wait a little while longer before getting back on the road for real, although most of our regular haunts hadn't yet resumed normal schedules anyway meaning there wasn't a meaningful gig circuit to join.

Looking back, this forced break came at the right time, because Liam had made a decision that would give me a problem that was to take some time to resolve.

He told me he had decided to stop gigging for the foreseeable future and concentrate on a career in teaching.

Of course, Carole and I were fully supportive of his decision, although sad to see him go, and we began the search for someone to take his place — Liam was a hard act to follow.

Initially, I turned to an old friend, Paul Burgess, who's main band is 10cc, although as their touring schedule is planned well in advance there were gaps where Paul would be available.
Paul drove down from his home in the northwest to rehearse with Roger and I and of course it sounded great!

Sighs of relief all round, although I knew at the outset that there would be many times when he would be busy with 10cc, meaning we still needed someone of the right calibre to fill the gaps.

It was June 2021 when we played Tring Court Theatre, beginning a regular gigging schedule although there have been many casualties, with clubs and theatres across the country unable to recover from the enforced break.

Liam played with us at Tring, and then Paul Burgess took over for our following shows at the 'Legends of Rock' Festival, and the 'Great British Blues Festival'. Then we got down to the task of finding someone to cover the shows that Paul would be unable to do.

Many phone calls later, someone said, "have you tried Kev Hickman?"

Kev is a brilliant drummer, who plays mainly with the band Catfish, which features the amazing guitarist Matt Long, and I was curious to see if he had any gaps in his diary, so gave him a call.

Kev said he'd love to play in my band, but was fully committed, as Catfish were really busy at the time, however he knew someone who he felt would be right for the job — Chris Mansbridge.

A call to Chris arranged a rehearsal, I sent some recordings of our material for him to learn and waited with trepidation to see what the outcome would be.

No need to worry, Roger and I were blown away by Chris's playing, he's brilliant, dead right for the band and a lovely guy to boot. Problem solved; we had our new drummer.

Chris has become our main drummer, with Paul's schedule with 10cc keeping him busy, although we did end up using Kev Hickman when Chris was otherwise engaged, so all's well that ends well, so they say.

This Rock 'n' Roll Won't Last You Know!

27
A Welcome Surprise

One day I had a call from Steve Rodford, saying that he had been looking through some of his dad's old stuff and found a couple of things I might be interested in.

Since Jim's death in 2018, Steve hadn't been able to look through all of the things left behind but, on this day, he'd come across a couple of vinyl records in plain covers with Jim's writing on them.

As Steve began reading Jim's notes, I realised that he was holding the only copies of the lost Phoenix album from 1977, the album that CBS had refused to release, leading to us changing direction and eventually to split.

The original master tapes had long since gone, and these were probably acetates from when I had asked Ray Staff to do a test cut of mixes I would have just completed at Trident Studios, so that I could check what they sounded like on vinyl, at home.

I must have given them to Jim, as he liked to keep stuff like that — he was a bit of a hoarder, bless him!

I drove immediately to Steve's place in St Albans to pick up the discs and contacted my friend Matt White to see if he could help me resurrect the recordings.

The first task was to de-click and digitise the tracks so that I could remaster them for release, if possible, and I knew that Matt was the man to help.

There were two acetates, and one was in better condition than the other, so we went to work on that, cleaning it up, de-clicking it and eventually I was able to spend some time at home remastering it.

When we recorded the tracks originally, over forty years ago some of the production techniques I used were achieved in a way vastly different to how we do things these days.

For example, on the track 'You Got Soul' begins with a heavily phased drum fill, achieved by manipulating the heads on the multitrack tape machine as we mixed, and the backwards guitar solo is achieved by removing the multitrack tape from the machine, turning it around and playing it backwards as I played the solo hearing the song played backwards in my headphones.

The result is that when the tape was the played the right way round, the solo was backwards. Nowadays, a simple click the computer mouse would reverse a guitar solo almost instantly.

One of the tracks on this album is Chris White's 'When My Boat Comes In'.

It's one of those songs that gives you goose pimples as you sing it, it's simply beautiful, and I'm so glad we had a chance to release it in the end, another chance to hear Rod's lovely piano part too.

At the end of this process you really couldn't tell it from the original recordings and the result is a pristine CD, released as *Phoenix – Out Of The Sun*, a title that Jim has written on the cover of the acetate we had used.

In order to fund the manufacture of the CD I turned to my 'JV Backstage' people, asking for donations in return for a mention on the CD cover, and for an 'executive producer' credit in return for a larger donation.

Phil Lightwood-Jones, Steve Rossi, Colin and Jacqui Dixon, Sandy Reid, Vikki Sheward, Lynne Birrell and David Cox came up with goods and the lost Phoenix album finally came out in 2021.

As we tried to get back to some kind of 'normal' I decided to record a new JV CD, even though we were still promoting *Passion* as our current offering.

I had been chatting to Max about the possibility of getting back together to do acoustic versions of some of my songs previously recorded as full JV Band tracks.

I really wanted to see if the songs would stand up in a stripped-down acoustic format, played by Max and Roger and myself.

Roger is an excellent upright bass player, although we had never recorded him doing that and I was curious as to how it would sound, with Max and me playing acoustic guitar parts.

I thought a four-track CD EP would fit the bill, and chose the songs to work on, all recorded previously by the band:

- Blues in Heaven
- Broken Heart
- A Better Way
- I Just Don't Love You Anymore

I knew that Max's slide guitar playing would really suite some of these, and along with Roger's upright bass would bring something a little different to the JV catalogue.

We did the sessions for *Blue* at my place over a short period and the CD was released in 2022. It was received really well by our hardcore of fans as I had hoped, and because it was so different it didn't seem to detract from our current promotion of Passion.

Incidentally, very few people seem to realise that *'I Just Don't Love You Anymore'* is not about my relationship with a person, it's actually about my relationship with a country!

I Just Don't Love You Anymore

You were my inspiration, everything to me
You were my inspiration, everything to me
How come so many apples fell so far from the tree

Well you talk about freedom, that ain't what I see
I hear you talk about freedom, that ain't what I see
Whatever it is, sure don't look like freedom to me
You say that change is gonna come, you'll back on the right track
You say that change is gonna come, you'll back on the right track
But will you ever get over the shame of looking back (I don't think so)

I just don't love you anymore.
(John Verity, Verity Music)

This Rock 'n' Roll Won't Last You Know!

28
New Horizons

Things were slowly picking up in 2022, although there had been permanent casualties on the gig front, with some of our old favourite haunts no longer functioning.

There seemed to be changes afoot in terms of audience expectations too, making it harder for bands like mine, playing a lot of original music in the live set to survive, although the JV Band was still working regularly despite this.

A promoter who I know well, Peter Barton had often suggested that it might be interesting for me to team up with another guitar player that I respected and put together a project to run alongside the JV Band, and although the idea did interest me I couldn't think of anyone to approach about the idea.

As it happens, Pete had recently had the same conversation with Del Bromham, who despite still gigging with his band Stray agreed it might be an interesting idea to call me, as Pete had suggested.

Del's call came at the right time to be honest; I can't imagine ever abandoning the JV Band but running something interesting alongside seemed a great option if it felt right.

Del and I agreed to get together at my place and pretty soon it became obvious that we should give it a shot and put a new band together to play our own arrangements of some popular material that we both liked.

All the songs had to be strong, and would feature us both on lead vocals, sharing guitar duties and just generally having a great time.

I asked JV Band drummer Chris Mansbridge to join us, and Del asked current Stray bassist Colin Kempster — 'Curvy' to his mates, to come onboard.

One rehearsal, we knew it was going to work and the Verity Bromham band was born!

We called Peter Barton with the news, and right away he gave us our first gig, 'The Great British Rhythm and Blues Festival' in Colne, Lancashire on 27th August 2022, where we were booked to do a one hour show at the Municipal Theatre in the town centre.

Not a lot was said in the dressing room prior to the gig, and although Del and I had been around the block and got the proverbial T-shirt I think we were both apprehensive, not wanting to say anything yet.

Soon it was time for our show, and I proceeded to get my gear set up and ready as I had thousands of times before, glancing across at Del, at the other side of the stage doing the same, and soon we were ready.

The MC introduced us, and we were off, to an immediate reaction that I'm sure shocked both of us as the audience took to what we were doing right away, probably much better than we both expected.

The four of us played really well together, and it sure didn't sound or feel like a new band's first show at all, this was good, really good.

We left the stage and headed for the dressing room, and I'll never forget looking at Del looking at me with the same expression — 'what on earth happened there?'

It was a great start, and a scene repeated at our next shows at Carlisle Blues Festival, Tivoli Theatre, and one of our favourites The Stables Theatre in Wavendon, Milton Keynes.

It soon became obvious that we needed recorded product for the new band and with that in mind I began putting together some bits of spare equipment to create a portable recording setup that I could take to gigs and make some live recordings of the show.

I felt that in view of the reaction we were getting at our gigs, a live album would be great.

In the meantime, we were due to play 'The Tuesday Night Music Club' in Coulsdon Surrey, a thriving venue run by promoter Richard Dunning, and on arrival I asked the sound guy, Ross Davey if he could make a rough recording of the show for me.

I was aware that we might occasionally need to use a different bassist or drummer if our guys weren't available, and I would need recording of our set to send to them so they could learn the songs.

Ross responded by saying he could record the set multi-track if I wanted and for a small fee, he would let me have the recordings to mix at home. Perfect! This might be a shortcut to our live album if the quality of the recording was good.

The show went really well, the audience were really up for it, and we had a great gig, although I hadn't told the guys it was being recorded.

I asked Ross to send me a short, five-minute snatch of one of the songs so I could see if the quality was good enough before committing to buy the whole thing.

A few days later, Ross's WeTransfer came in and I downloaded the files, loaded them into my music software and was amazed to hear a near-perfect recording of one of the songs in our set.

I couldn't believe our luck, we might have our first album on its way already, all I had to do was get the files from Ross, mix, and master them, sort out some artwork and we'd be good to go.

Del had already told me that a couple of professional photographers had been at the show, so there might be some shots that we could use for the cover, and if they didn't work out other photographers from earlier shows had begun to get in touch.

In the end we were able to use great live shots taken by Manuela Langotsch, Tony Cole, Haluk Gurer, and Ken Jackson.

Reaction to the CD has been amazing, and my lovely missus Carole is working hard on getting work for Verity Bromham and The JV Band moving forward.

This Rock 'n' Roll Won't Last You Know!

29
Not Quite 'The End'

It's 2023. Del and I are looking forward to good times ahead with Verity Bromham, and the John Verity Band is alive and kicking with current lineup of Chris Mansbridge on drums and Roger Inniss on bass.

In my personal life I'm blessed, with an amazing wife Carole who puts up with my obsession with music and all things musical with no complaints.

I have a huge pile of regrets, I guess that comes with the territory, and there's no way to go back and fix my mistakes, sadly.

I guess I'll just 'keep on keeping on', as they say.

There are unsung heroes without whom I wouldn't be able to keep on my never-ending quest for 'tone', Phil and Sam Taylor at *Effectrode Thermionic*, Tim Mills at *Bare Knuckle Pickups*, John Dixon at *Scott Dixon*, and last but not least the amazing Trev Wilkinson.

I'm lucky to have worked and played with some of the best, many of them sadly no longer with us, although I still have my memories.

Like many professional musicians I've been through difficult times recently that began with Brexit, then the Covid-19 Pandemic, both of which had disastrous effects on our industry.

Again, like most professionals I'm not going to let these setbacks stop me, there's too much good music to play, with good people... to good people.

So, things are looking good, and we're doing our best to Keep Our Music Alive — although this Rock 'n' Roll won't last you know!

This Rock 'n' Roll Won't Last You Know!